D0886815

A Right to Discriminate?

A Right to Discriminate?

How the Case of Boy Scouts of America v. James Dale
Warped the Law of Free Association

Andrew Koppelman with
Tobias Barrington Wolff

Yale University Press   New Haven and London

Published with assistance from the foundation established in memory of Henry Weldon Barnes of the Class of 1882, Yale College.

Set in Galliard type by Keystone Typesetting, Inc., Orwigsburg, Pennsylvania.
Printed in the United States of America by Sheridan Books, Ann Arbor, Michigan.

Library of Congress Cataloging-in-Publication Data
Koppelman, Andrew.
   A right to discriminate? : how the case of Boy Scouts of America v. James Dale warped the law of free association / Andrew Koppelman with Tobias Barrington Wolff.
      p. cm.
   Includes bibliographical references and index.
   ISBN 978-0-300-12127-8 (cloth : alk. paper)
   1. Freedom of association — United States. 2. Discrimination — Law and legislation — United States. 3. Associations, institutions, etc. — Law and legislation — United States. 4. Boy Scouts — Legal status, laws, etc. — United States. 5. Gays — Legal status, laws, etc. — United States. 6. Boy Scouts of America — Trials, litigation, etc. 7. Dale, James — Trials, litigation, etc. 8. Federal aid to higher education — United States. I. Wolff, Tobias Barrington. II. Title.
   KF4778.K67 2009
   342.7308'54 — dc22

A catalogue record for this book is available from the British Library.

This paper meets the requirements of ANSI/NISO Z39.48-1992 (Permanence of Paper). It contains 30 percent postconsumer waste (PCW) and is certified by the Forest Stewardship Council (FSC).

10 9 8 7 6 5 4 3 2 1

Contents

For Ruby Lee Koppelman and Howard Lee, with whom I'm proud to be associated.

A.K.

To the many students who struggled for dignity and equality in the Solomon Amendment litigation. Our differences on constitutional doctrine and tactics are behind us, and our common vision of equal citizenship remains.

T.W.

Acknowledgments

This book began when Michael McConnell, the counsel for the Boy Scouts of America in the *Dale* case, asked Andrew Koppelman to consider publicly supporting the BSA's position in that case. McConnell, a brilliant attorney (and now a judge on the U.S. Court of Appeals for the Tenth Circuit), knew that Koppelman had published a number of arguments supporting gay rights and thought it would be helpful to his case if Koppelman were persuaded to support a right to discriminate in this context. Koppelman saw the force of McConnell's arguments and was still deciding what position to take when he spoke with Tobias Wolff, who argued the other side so forcefully that Koppelman was converted. Once interested in the issue, Koppelman began the research that has culminated in this book. Meanwhile, Wolff was following and writing prominently about the *FAIR* case, and our conversations made clear to us that we took the same view of the merits. Wolff is responsible primarily for Chapter 3, but his influence on this book is pervasive. We are both grateful to Judge McConnell for his role in bringing into existence a book with which he remains in profound disagreement.

Thanks to Marcia Lehr for first-class research assistance, and to Yale University Press copyeditor Jessie Dolch, who went above and beyond the call of duty and rescued us from several major errors. Thanks, also, to Yale University Press editor Michael O'Malley, who helped us devise the title. Special thanks to David Bernstein, Risa Goluboff, and Joseph Singer for commenting on a draft of Chapter 1 with very short notice.

Portions of this book previously appeared in the following articles:

Andrew Koppelman, *Signs of the Times: Dale v. Boy Scouts of America and the Changing Meaning of Nondiscrimination*, 23 Cardozo Law Rev. 1819 (2002).

Andrew Koppelman, *Are the Boy Scouts Being as Bad as Racists? Judging the Scouts' Antigay Policy*, 18 Pub. Aff. Q. 363 (2004).

Andrew Koppelman, *Should Noncommercial Associations Have an Absolute Right to Discriminate?*, 67 Law and Contemp. Problems 27 (Aut. 2004).

Tobias Barrington Wolff and Andrew Koppelman, *Expressive Association and the Ideal of the University in the Solomon Amendment Litigation*, 25 Soc. Phil. & Pol'y 92 (2008).

Introduction

James Dale joined the Boy Scouts of America (BSA) when he was eight years old. He had wanted to join when he was even younger because his older brother and his father were members. He was an enthusiastic Scout, rising to the rank of Eagle, the highest honor the BSA bestows. "Boy Scouts was community," he later explained. "It was a place where I felt I belonged. I did other things. I was in soccer and basketball. But nothing fit as well as the Boy Scouts. I felt I didn't have to be the best football player or run the fastest. In the Boy Scouts, I could be who I was. They valued me for who I was."[1]

When he turned eighteen, his membership automatically expired, but he was invited to remain in the organization as an assistant Scoutmaster. Then, when he went to college, he learned about the local gay community and decided to come out as gay. He joined the school's lesbian and gay organization during his sophomore year and within three months had become its copresident. A picture of him appeared in the local newspaper in a story about a gay youth workshop. The article did not mention his membership in the BSA.

The BSA, after seeing the story, sent Dale a letter expelling him from the organization. The letter did not explain the reason for the expulsion. When he wrote to inquire why, he was told that the BSA "specifically forbid[s] membership to homosexuals." In all his years as a Boy Scout, he had never heard of any such policy, and, he told an interviewer later, "it was like a kidney punch. I felt betrayed. This was the organization that taught me how to be me."[2] Dale sued the BSA under New Jersey's antidiscrimination law. He prevailed in the New Jersey Supreme Court but ultimately lost in the U.S. Supreme Court. The Court held that the BSA had a constitutional right to exclude Dale.

What sort of right is this? Where did it come from? The question of whether the BSA should have won its case is an interesting one, but it is also connected to another and more momentous question: should associations have a constitutional right to discriminate in their membership? If so, what should the scope of this right be?

Until 2000, the answer to these questions in American law was clear. Associations that conveyed messages were entitled to be free of restrictions, including restrictions on their membership practices, that interfered with the dissemination of those messages. Intimate associations of small groups of people had a stronger right, to refuse association with anyone for any reason. Outside of these limitations, freedom of association could not be invoked by a defendant to defeat the operation of an antidiscrimination law. Most antidiscrimination laws are of limited scope — for example, there is usually an exemption for businesses with a small number of employees — but this is a matter of legislative discretion rather than constitutional principle.

Two recent Supreme Court cases have muddied the law. In James

Dale's case, *Boy Scouts of America v. Dale*,[3] the Court ruled that the BSA had a right to discriminate against gay members. In *Rumsfeld v. Forum for Academic and Institutional Rights (FAIR)*,[4] the Court rejected a claim that law schools had a right to exclude recruiters from the military, which openly discriminates against gays, from their campuses. These two cases have left the law in confusion. *Dale* implied that all antidiscrimination laws were constitutionally vulnerable; *FAIR* restricted the scope of *Dale* to an uncertain extent.

The confusion *Dale* created is not only legal. The litigation has also created a crisis of cultural status for the BSA. Since the litigation highlighted the BSA's antigay policy, membership has dropped. The reaction against the BSA provokes questions about how, if at all, citizens ought to respond to this kind of discrimination.

The ambitions of this book are fundamentally conservative. Before *Dale*, there was a well-settled law of freedom of association. *Dale* has disrupted that law, capriciously and destructively. This book is a plea for the restoration of the *ancien regime*.

Before *Dale*, the treatment of freedom of association by American constitutional law followed what has been called a "message-based approach": if an association is organized to express a viewpoint, then constitutional difficulties are raised by a statute that requires it to accept unwanted members if that requirement would impair its ability to convey its message. It was on the basis of this rule that the New Jersey Supreme Court had decided against the BSA, finding that Scouting was not organized around any message concerning sexuality. This rule has become unclear because *Dale* introduced two key ambiguities into the law. First, it seemed to hold that substantial interference would be assumed to exist whenever an organization asserted this position in a lawsuit. Second, it seemed to hold that substantial burdens were per se unconstitutional, rather than merely subject to strict scrutiny. This logic leads to such silly results that the lower federal courts have refused to believe it. The message-based approach lives.

A notable group of commentators, whom we shall call the "neolibertarians," have responded to *Dale*'s ambiguity by advocating a sharper rule than any declared in the *Dale* opinion: an absolute right of noncommercial associations to exclude unwanted members. (The restriction of the right to noncommercial associations is what makes them "neo.") The neolibertarians object to a message-based approach because they think it gives government the opportunity to scrutinize and reshape private speech, and thereby violates the central purposes of the First Amendment. One illustration of the pathology of a message-based approach, emphasized by several of these writers and by the *Dale* Court as well, is that it produces perverse results: a group that is stridently prejudiced will receive more protection than one that is quieter about its views, and thus the rule creates an incentive to disseminate the precise prejudices that antidiscrimination laws aim to temper.

The neolibertarian arguments are, however, only slightly modified versions of old, discredited libertarian objections to the existence of any antidiscrimination law at all. The older, minimal-state libertarianism rests on three premises: (1) that a more-than-minimal state violates citizens' rights, (2) that government cannot be trusted to do more than prevent force and fraud, and (3) that an unregulated private sector can be relied on to produce benign results. Libertarianism has failed as a normative theory because all three premises are often false. The neolibertarian modification is to confine these three premises so that they apply only to noncommercial associations. But even thus restricted in scope, there is no reason to think that any of them is true as a general matter.

What the neolibertarians describe as perverse effects of a message-based approach are actually desirable ones. The pressure that a message-based approach brings to bear on discriminatory associations is exactly the kind of result that antidiscrimination law should strive to bring about, and it reaches it in a way that gives freedom of speech all the respect that it deserves. Discrimination is not so cheap as it was before, and a group will have to decide whether discrimination is worth the added cost. But this pressure serves state interests of the highest order and does not prevent groups with strongly held discriminatory ideas from uniting and disseminating them.

All of the recent agitation for a judicially broadened freedom of association is misguided. The basic problem is analogous to the problem of how much economic regulation there should be. The arguments for free markets are not only economic. Unregulated economic interaction can also promote powerful virtues of character. But after the case has been made against Communism as an economic system, an enormous range of possibilities remains, and the rejection of Stalinist centralism tells us little about the case for any particular regulation. Similarly, even if it is hugely important that there be a great deal of unregulated association, very little follows about the boundary between the regulated and the unregulated. It certainly does not follow that this boundary ought to be determined by the courts, which is what a constitutional right amounts to in practice.

The BSA case illustrates the importance of allowing the state to pursue legitimate antidiscrimination interests. The discriminatory policy hurts the youth who participate in Scouting. It is not endorsed by many BSA members, and there is no reason automatically to take the side of the BSA leadership in this internal dispute. The state also has a legitimate interest in making sure that one of the central institutions of the socialization of youth — as a matter of fact, the largest youth organization in the country — is available to all boys in a non-discriminatory fashion and is not torn apart by a rash decision to join in the culture wars.[5]

Chapter 1 examines the case law on free association up to the *Dale* case. Chapter 2 scrutinizes the reasoning in *Dale*. Chapter 3 examines the Court's latest foray into the freedom of association question in *FAIR,* concluding that the Court in that case restrained the worst excesses of *Dale* while leaving the law fundamentally unsettled. Chapter 4 addresses the neolibertarian proposal. Chapters 5 and 6 look more closely at the BSA's policy to try to discern whether it presents a problem that the state can legitimately address. Chapter 5 argues that the policy is, in pertinent ways, the moral equivalent of racial discrimination. Chapter 6 offers further reasons for intervention: the rule laid down by *Dale* is likely to harm youth, systematically frustrate parents' preferences, and impair the BSA from performing just those mediating functions of associations that the defenders of free association are eager to protect.

I

Origins of the Right to Exclude

This book examines the idea that there is a freedom of association that creates a right to resist antidiscrimination law.[1] Where did this idea come from? There are two answers to this question because the idea of a right to exclude has two sources. One of these, the older of the two, is broadly libertarian. The newer source is narrower, rooted in the First Amendment's protection of free speech.

The earlier, libertarian rationale implies such a broad right to exclude that it is inconsistent with nearly any antidiscrimination law. Some courts adopted it, but this was an innovation of the Civil War period, devised specifically in order to authorize discrimination against African Americans. It has never transcended its maculate provenance. The free speech rationale is not so tainted and can provide a basis for limiting antidiscrimination law. But this basis generates a fairly narrow right to exclude.

The Libertarian Right to Exclude

The central claim of libertarianism, the philosophy of a minimal, laissez-faire state, is that government ought not to intervene in the private sector because to do so violates citizens' rights, because government cannot be trusted with such powers, or because the unregulated private sector is already the best of all possible worlds. Libertarianism in its classic form — call it "paleolibertarianism," to distinguish it from the neolibertarianism of the contemporary writers whom I address in Chapter 4 — rests on three claims, which I will call "Rights," "Distrust," and "Optimism."

The Rights claim is that laws against discrimination are unjust regardless of what the consequences of discrimination might be. It resembles Kantian deontology in that it insists on economic rights without depending on predictions about the workings of an unregulated economy.[2]

It begins with the premise that law should not interfere with liberty except to prevent violations of rights. Interferences for any reason other than the prevention of rights violations are themselves rights violations. When *A* associates with *B* but refuses to associate with *C*, that association does not violate any rights of *C*. No one has a right to compel others to associate with another one. Therefore, *A* has a right not to associate with *C*. It follows that the law violates *A*'s rights when it penalizes *A* for his or her refusal to associate with *C*. When a state violates people's rights, it fails to show them the respect to which they are entitled.[3]

Theories of this kind are familiar in the liberal tradition, but they rest on a remarkably constricted account of the human interests that the state can legitimately protect.[4] A society could, on this account, have a permanent outcast population in a state of chronic economic misery, vulnerable to ruthless exploitation,[5] and the state would have no power to remedy this situation, even if the culture of prejudice that is maintained thereby is one that itself produces numerous rights violations.[6] The social world that libertarianism envisions is not a society of free and equal persons. Rather, it resembles feudalism: the poor and weak must place themselves under the protection of the rich and strong, on whatever terms the latter are willing to grant.[7]

It is bizarre to think that respect for people demands such person-destroying results. Not only does this account fetishize a historically contingent distribution of entitlements; it also misreads the history it fetishizes. As we shall see shortly, the idea that property entails an absolute right to discriminate is not embedded in the common law from time immemorial but is an artifact of the Jim Crow era. Immanuel Kant, who is the wellspring of such rights-based arguments, was not himself so indifferent to considerations of human welfare.[8]

Another strand of libertarian thought does attend to consequences. It rests on two interdependent claims: that government is not to be trusted (Distrust), and that an unregulated capitalist economy produces good results (Optimism).[9] The claims are interdependent because the strength of each depends on that of the other: even a largely self-regulating economy might usefully be tinkered with by a sufficiently wise and trustworthy government, whereas if an unregulated economy leads to disaster, even an incompetent and corrupt regulator may be better than no regulator at all.

Both claims are exaggerated. The idea that capitalist economies can regulate themselves may have been plausible in John Locke's time, but it is hardly so in ours.[10] Unregulated markets do not distribute goods in a just way.[11] Their capacity to satisfy people's preferences is routinely hamstrung by monopolies, externalities, collective action problems, information asymmetries, and other market failures. They also produce aggregate effects that no one wants, such as vicious cycles of boom and bust. This is why libertarianism has been such a flop. No unregulated economy exists in any modern industrial country. And government has not proved to be all that untrustworthy. After the judiciary stopped reading libertarianism into the Constitution in the 1930s, the U.S. economy did not collapse, but rather was able to rely on its economic output to win World War II and the Cold War. Central management of the money supply has produced a marked softening of the business cycle. Libertarians worry about regulators being captured by powerful interests, but much of modern regulation manages to pursue the public interest.[12] The classic tales of wasteful overregulation that are repeatedly cited in the media have been proved apocryphal.[13] As a general matter, experience falsifies both Optimism and Distrust.

They meet the same fate when they are applied to antidiscrimination law. Richard Epstein has argued that consumer welfare would be maximized if a right to discriminate were allowed.[14] Epstein's optimism about the fate of minorities in unrestricted markets is one that is supported neither by history nor by economic theory.[15] Once more, the premise of Distrust is called into question by the success of antidiscrimination laws in dismantling discriminatory markets and opening economic opportunities to black citizens. Before the Civil Rights Act of 1964, unregulated markets had perpetuated race discrimination for decades, and the act, far from being incompetent meddling in a thriving economy, produced a huge decrease in the disparity between black and white incomes.[16]

There is, of course, a valid core to libertarianism. Markets generate wealth better than any rival economic arrangement. They are distributively just insofar as they make the availability of resources to any person depend on the value of those resources to others.[17] And they necessarily preclude some kinds of centralized direction: "Freedom means that in some measure we entrust our fate to forces which we do not control."[18] But these generalizations have important exceptions. In the face of market failures, state intervention is appropriate. Courts have learned that they are not very good at deciding whether these conditions obtain in any given case, so they generally stay out of the regulation question and leave it to the political branches, the virtues of free markets notwithstanding. There is a big difference between being right most of the time and being right all of the time. Einstein showed that Newton was right most of the time.

Origins of the Libertarian Right

If the libertarian claim is so weak, why has it had such a powerful hold on Americans' imaginations? Why would anyone think that there is an absolute right to discriminate?

The idea of a legal prohibition against discrimination is as old as the United States.[19] At common law before the Civil War, every business that held itself out as open to serve the public arguably had a legal obligation to serve anyone who sought service. The range of businesses that held this obligation is not clear. The legal authorities expressly extended the duty only to inns, blacksmiths, and common carriers, such as trains. But an exhaustive survey finds that "legal authority for the proposition that businesses other than common carriers and innkeepers have a right to serve whomever they wish is sparse to nonexistent."[20] The reasons given for the duty were almost always that these businesses had held themselves out as ready to serve anyone, and that they could therefore be treated as "common callings" with a duty to provide service. This logic obviously applies to all businesses open to the public.[21]

The rule had a limited scope. Boardinghouses, for example, which rented rooms on a more permanent basis than inns, were exempt from the duty to serve the public.[22] But this limit was not a matter of constitutional right. It was just where the nondiscrimination obligation stopped. There was no reason to think that the courts would have interfered if the obligation had been extended further by statute.

This rule's sphere of application began to constrict around the time of the Civil War, when legal rights were for the first time extended to African Americans. At that point, courts changed the rule without saying that they were doing so. They held for the first time that most businesses had no common-law duty to serve the public. At the same time, some legislatures specifically abrogated that duty.[23] This was the origin of the rule that now prevails throughout the United States. The Iowa Supreme Court's 1885 declaration of the right to exclude arose in the case of an establishment that refused to admit black customers:

> It may be said, as a general rule, that the law does not under-
> take to govern or regulate the citizen in the conduct of his pri-
> vate business. In all matters of mere private concern he is left
> free to deal with whom he pleases, and to make such bargains
> as he is able to make with those with whom he does deal.[24]

The Iowa court held that inns still had an obligation not to discriminate, but only five years later, the North Carolina Supreme Court declared that even innkeepers could exclude people who are "so objectionable to the patrons of the house, on account of the race to which they belong, that it would injure the business to admit them to all portions of the house."[25]

The libertarian right to exclude, then, is racist at the core. This change in the law had the purpose, clear on the face of some of the opinions, of permitting businesses to refuse service to African Americans.

Joseph Singer observes that this shift in the common-law rule should not be understood as the lifting of a regulation of property. On the contrary, it amounted to a forcible transfer of property rights:

> The courts . . . took a property right belonging to the public —
> an easement of access to businesses open to the public with a
> concomitant duty on businesses to serve the public — and re-
> placed it with a business right to exclude correlative with no
> right of access by members of the public, unless the business fit
> into a narrow range of public service companies.[26]

At the same time that it was expanding businesses' right to exclude, the courts upheld laws that required racial segregation of customers, which was an unprecedented intrusion on businesses' property rights.[27] The courts held that these were reasonable regulations.

In a remarkable argumentative move, the courts sometimes justified these regulations in terms of freedom of association. Since white customers did not want to associate with black ones, they reasoned, the segregation rules upheld whites' freedom of association. Thus, in 1867 the Pennsylvania Supreme Court justified a railroad's forcible segregation of its passengers on this ground. The court regarded the "feeling of aversion between individuals of the different races" as a fact of life. "If a negro take his seat beside a white man or his wife or daughter, the law cannot repress the anger, or conquer the aversion which some will feel."[28] It concluded that

> following the order of Divine Providence, human authority
> ought not to compel these widely separated races to intermix.
> The right of such to be free from social contact is as clear as to
> be free from intermarriage. The former may be less repulsive as

a condition, but not less entitled to protection as a right. When, therefore, we declare a right to maintain separate relations, as far as is reasonably practicable, but in a spirit of kindness and charity, and with due regard to equality of rights, it is not prejudice, nor caste, nor injustice of any kind, but simply to suffer men to follow the law of races established by the Creator himself, and not to compel them to intermix contrary to their instincts.[29]

The Supreme Court made the same argument in 1896 in *Plessy v. Ferguson,* in which the Court upheld a statute requiring segregation of rail cars. It, too, denounced "an enforced commingling of the two races."[30]

This is a strange argument because it indicates that association is being "compelled" unless segregation is forcibly imposed. That imposition, of course, affirmatively bars association by whites and blacks who do want to associate with one another. Nonetheless, as we shall see, the "forced association" defense of segregation persisted for a long time.

The argument becomes more intelligible if one brings forth the background assumption that any reasonable white person *would* want to discriminate — that the desire to be free from having to associate with blacks is a natural and normal part of being white. This is reflected in the Pennsylvania court's invocation of the "feeling of aversion" as a matter of natural "instincts." Call this the "pariah assumption"; we shall encounter it again. There is a tension within this view, since the "instinct" in question increasingly appears to need policing and reinforcement. As C. Vann Woodward noted long ago, the program of Jim Crow denounced Reconstruction as a futile attempt to change supposedly immutable social mores, while it was itself an elaborate and ambitious program of social engineering.[31]

Eventually, the expanded common-law right to discriminate very nearly became constitutionalized. The Court in the late nineteenth century was drawn toward a libertarian line of reasoning. The most charitable reading of this libertarianism would hold that the capacity to buy and sell one's labor was the central ideological basis of the Civil War.[32] The Thirteenth and Fourteenth Amendments, on this reading, centrally stood for nonslavery, and nonslavery centrally meant the right to own property and to freedom of contract. Rights of property and contract must presuppose some baseline. I have to know what my rights are before I can know whether the state is infringing on them. If property and contract are merely whatever the law says they are, then there are no rights, independent of the positive law, to infringe. The courts responded to this problem by taking as the baseline common-law rights. Whenever a law infringed on liberty or property without adequate justification, it was unconstitutionally depriving people of liberty or property without due process of law. As the common-law baseline shifted, so did the scope of constitutionally protected liberty.

This tendency began as early as 1856,[33] and it received the imprimatur of the Supreme Court in 1905. In *Lochner v. New York,*[34] the Court struck down a maximum-hours law as an unwarranted interference with freedom of contract. The Court thereafter struck down a wide range of regulations of business for interfering with economic liberty. Racial segregation ordinances remained untouched, but now there was a colorable argument that a law prohibiting discrimination violated rights of property and contract by forcing people to enter into economic associations that they did not desire.

In the late 1800s, laws banning racial discrimination in public accommodations were enacted in many states, reflecting the political power of black voters.[35] These laws were attacked on freedom of association grounds as early as the 1870s. Challengers repeatedly argued that antidiscrimination laws were unconstitutional interferences with property and contract. The arguments were plausible inferences from libertarian principles, but they never prevailed.[36]

In the earliest of these, *Donnell v. State* (1873),[37] the defendant in a discrimination case claimed that a seat in a concert hall was "an article, not of necessity, but simply of luxury; an article which he has a constitutional right to sell at any price he pleases, or to whom he pleases."[38] The existence of racism was an independent justification for such discrimination:

> The white race do not desire to drink out of the same vessel, to
> eat out of the same plate, or to sleep in the same bed with
> them, or to sit in places of amusement, in the dress circle of
> theatres with them. And it is as unwise as it is unconstitutional
> for the legislature of the state to attempt to control those mat-
> ters of taste by legislative enactment.[39]

The Mississippi Supreme Court rejected these arguments, holding that the law was a valid exercise of the police power. It also noted that at common law, "all who applied for admission to the public shows and amusements, were entitled to admission, and in each instance, for a refusal, an action on the case lay, unless sufficient reason were shown."[40]

The Mississippi court disclaimed any reliance on the "utility and expediency" of the law in question. Fifteen years later, however, the New York Court of Appeals went further, arguing that an antidiscrimination law protects the equality of black citizens: "It is evident that to exclude colored people from places of public resort on account of their race, is to fix upon them a brand of inferiority, and tends to fix their position as a servile and dependent people."[41]

Nonetheless, freedom of contract concerns did lead courts to construe these statutes narrowly, frequently refusing to extend coverage to any entity not specifically named in the statute, even if the law broadly reached all "places of public accommodation." The grudging enforcement of the statutes by the courts helped keep racial discrimination ubiquitous.[42]

At about the same time, in 1908, the idea of a constitutional freedom of association was strongly suggested by the Supreme Court in *Berea College v. Kentucky*,[43] in which it upheld the application of a statute prohibiting private schools from teaching white and black pupils in the same building. The Court conceded that the statute "may conflict with the Federal Constitution in denying to individuals powers which they may rightfully exercise,"[44] but held that the state's plenary authority over corporations meant that it could deny to corporations, such as the defendant in the case, those powers. Justice John Marshall Harlan dissented on grounds of statutory interpretation but agreed with the Court that citizens had a right of "voluntary meeting for innocent purposes."[45] If there was a right to voluntarily associate, this might imply a right to exclude. This implication was never pursued, however.

A few other decisions during this period suggest a right to association. *Buchanan v. Warley* (1917) declared unconstitutional a law that prevented blacks from purchasing homes in white neighborhoods.[46] In *Meyer v. Nebraska* (1923), the Court invalidated a law prohibiting the teaching of any language other than English.[47] In *Pierce v. Society of Sisters* (1925), the Court struck down a law requiring children to attend public schools, which would effectively have destroyed all the private schools in the state.[48] All of these, in different ways, created rights to resist the state's power to force private associations to conform to a government-imposed norm.

The Supreme Court did not address the issue of a right to discriminate until 1945, in *Railway Mail Ass'n v. Corsi*.[49] At issue was the application of an antidiscrimination law to an all-white labor union. The union represented its members in disputes with the employer; its members had a contractual right to appeal their grievances to the head of their department; and they also received low-cost accident insurance from their union. The union emphasized its character as a private association:

> The question of discrimination when applied to the case at bar is a sociological matter which, in the absence of a constitutional grant from the people to the government, cannot be regulated under the State Police Powers. Such discrimination is not unjust. It is a preference causing no injustice to anyone. It concerns a social relationship which must rest on voluntary action. The law cannot coerce its performance. We are all left free to choose. This is a personal and constitutional right beyond the power of legislation. The choice is inherent in the person. Tolerance may broaden the choice and benevolence may soften to the point of common acceptance. Education and the spirit of Christianity may efface the thought of social differences. Coercive legislation is not the remedy.[50]

The Supreme Court was unimpressed. It responded, first, that the Fourteenth Amendment was intended to combat, rather than abet, racism. "A judicial determination that such legislation violated the Fourteenth Amendment would be a distortion of the policy manifested in that amendment which was adopted to prevent state legislation designed to perpetuate discrimination on the basis of race or color."[51] Second, the exclusion was hardly harmless, given the power that labor unions possessed.

> To deny a fellow-employee membership because of race, color or creed may operate to prevent that employee from having any part in the determination of labor policies to be promoted and adopted in the industry and deprive him of all means of protection from unfair treatment arising out of the fact that the terms imposed by a dominant union apply to all employees, whether union members or not.[52]

Concern about the power of large associations led courts to be skeptical of a right to discriminate in other areas of the law. For example, it influenced the Court's interpretation of labor law. Faced with unions that were mostly white and hostile to African American membership, the Court in *Steele v. Louisville & N.R. Co.* in 1944 interpreted the Railway Labor Act to create a duty of fair representation, so that the white unions could not enter into discriminatory agreements that harmed black workers.[53] This created a peculiar kind of forced association. The unions were not forced to admit blacks — a provision to do so was abandoned during the drafting of the National Labor Relations Act for fear that it would scuttle the whole bill[54] — but they were obligated to treat them *as if* they were members, by representing their interests. In effect, white unions were required to accept blacks as semimembers.

The California Supreme Court went even further the following year, holding that when unions amassed sufficient power, they became quasi-public entities. In *James v. Marinship Corp.*, a shipbuilder's union admitted blacks only as members of an "auxiliary," with no voting powers or grievance committee. Black workers refused to join the auxiliary, and the union then sought to have the workers fired pursuant to a closed shop agreement. The union, anticipating an argument that would become prominent during the twenty-first century, argued that it "should not be compelled to admit all persons to membership, because some of such persons may have interests inimical to the union and may destroy it from within."[55] The court responded:

> Where a union has, as in this case, attained a monopoly of the supply of labor by means of closed shop agreements and other forms of collective labor action, such a union occupies a quasi public position similar to that of a public service business and it has certain corresponding obligations. It may no longer claim the same freedom from legal restraint enjoyed by golf clubs or fraternal associations.[56]

The court did not bar the union from discriminating. The union was not even a party to the litigation. But the court did effectively make unenforceable any racially discriminatory labor agreement. It thus rejected long-standing legal doctrine about the independence of unions from regulation.[57]

The question of a right to exclude arose in a different way in the White Primary cases, in which the Supreme Court confronted the persistent efforts of the Texas Democratic Party to prevent blacks from participating in elections.[58] The first laws that the Court struck down straightforwardly barred blacks from voting in any Democratic Party primary; later ones achieved the same result indirectly by giving the Democratic Party the power to prescribe its primary voters' qualifications. The Court held that all these stratagems amounted to discrimination practiced by the state, hence unconstitutional.

In *Smith v. Allwright* (1944),[59] the Court confronted an internal Democratic Party rule restricting membership in the party to whites. The party argued that it was a purely private association, "a voluntary association of persons of common political beliefs,"[60] and so immune from regulation. The Texas attorney general agreed. The First Amendment, he claimed, protected citizens' right to organize political parties, and more generally, "the privilege to create any kind of an organization they desired which does not violate the law."[61] The Court was unimpressed. It did not deign to respond to the First Amendment claim. A political party, the Court held, was "an agency of the State in so far as it determines the participants in a primary election."[62]

The most difficult of these cases, *Terry v. Adams* (1953),[63] invalidated the racially exclusive preprimary run by a private association, the "Jaybird Association." The association held a vote before the Democratic primary, with only white voters permitted to participate. The winner of the Jaybird vote invariably went on to win the general election. Once more, a First Amendment freedom of association was asserted.[64] The Court, however, held that this arrangement constituted state action and so violated the Fourteenth Amendment. The Court's reasoning, declared in three separate opinions, was not persuasive. The trouble was that the Jaybirds looked like a purely private association, not clothed with any formal state power.[65] But the Court, although fragmented about the rationale for its decision, understood that the "private" nature of the association masked a degree of power that could have an enormous influence on substantive constitutional rights. Once more, the Court would not deem an association private if it held so much substantive power.

Unhappily, the Court in *Terry* relied on a formalistic analysis of when "state action" could be found that evaded the hard functional questions presented by the case.[66] The hardest of these was how much substantive power an association had to have before it ceased to be "private" and immune from regulation. The Texas attorney general pressed this point vigorously:

> It seems to be urged that the right to participate in the party procedure exists where the party is always successful in procuring the election of its candidates. At what stage of the political life of a party would this "right" come into existence? Will success on the first occasion after the organization of the party give rise to the right, or must there be a longer period of gestation? If, after a long period of success, the party loses an election, is the right lost ? For what period does it remain dormant; how much success, after a loss, does it take to revive the right? If a party is always successful in Statewide elections, but not in particular district elections, does the "qualified elector" have the right to participate in the primary for the selection of candidates for the State-wide election but not for the selection of candidates for the district election?[67]

This problem would return. Since the Court had not said anything about the criterion for determining when an association became important enough to regulate, it created a space in which unstated assumptions could do a great deal of practical work.

Thereafter, the freedom of association argument against antidiscrimination law was dead in the courts. But it remained alive in the popular culture.

In 1959, in response to the Court's decision in *Brown v. Board of*

Education[68] that segregated schools were unconstitutional, Herbert Wechsler, in a widely cited article, resuscitated the old "forced association" justification for legally mandated racial segregation:

> But if the freedom of association is denied by segregation, integration forces an association upon those for whom it is unpleasant or repugnant. . . . Given a situation where the state must practically choose between denying the association to those individuals who wish it or imposing it on those who would avoid it, is there a basis in neutral principles for holding that the Constitution demands that the claims for association should prevail?[69]

The fundamental confusion here is made clear in a response to Wechsler by Charles Black. The freedom not to associate, Black observed, "exists only at home; in public, we have to associate with anybody who has a right to be there. The question of our right not to associate with him is concluded when we decide whether he has a right to be there."[70]

In 1964, the Republican presidential candidate, Senator Barry Goldwater, opposed the Civil Rights Act on precisely this basis, as did Ayn Rand, Robert Bork, and the young William Rehnquist (who would later write the Court's opinion in *Dale*).[71] But Congress passed the act, barring discrimination in employment and public accommodations, and the Supreme Court quickly dismissed claims that the act violated property rights.[72]

Origins of the Speech-Based Right

The Civil Rights Act did not, however, mean the end of the constitutional right to exclude. A new understanding of freedom of association was developing in a different form, resting on an entirely different basis.

The germinal case is *NAACP v. Alabama ex rel Patterson* (1958).[73] As part of their concerted resistance to desegregation and the enfranchisement of black voters, Alabama and other states invoked state corporation laws in an effort to compel the National Association for the Advancement of Colored People and its local affiliates to disclose the names of their members. In the atmosphere of intimidation and violence that prevailed in many quarters at the time, the organization asserted that compelled disclosure of its membership lists would effectively destroy the organization's ability to function by deterring members from contributing their money or their efforts to the organization's advocacy. As the Court explained, the NAACP had "made an uncontroverted showing that on past occasions revelation of the identity of its rank-and-file members [had] exposed these members to economic reprisal, loss of employment, threat of physical coercion, and other manifestations of public hostility."[74] The Court unanimously held that "[e]ffective advocacy of both public and private points of view, particularly controversial ones, is undeniably enhanced by group association." Speech and association were tightly connected: "[i]t is beyond debate that freedom to engage in association for the advancement of beliefs and ideas is an inseparable aspect of the . . . freedom of speech."[75] Alabama failed to show an interest in its generic disclosure laws that was sufficient to justify a threat to that freedom, and the NAACP was allowed to continue protecting its members' anonymity.[76]

NAACP v. Alabama made clear that freedom of association was firmly rooted in the First Amendment, but it did not address the right to exclude. This right was considered in 1976, and summarily rejected, in *Runyon v. McCrary*,[77] when the Court upheld the constitutionality of the Civil Rights Act of 1866 as applied to a private school that wished to remain all white and teach principles of segregation and white supremacy. While "it may be assumed that parents have a First Amendment right to send their children to educational institutions that promote the belief that racial segregation is desirable," the Court held, "it does not follow that the *practice* of excluding racial minorities from such institutions is also protected by the same principle."[78] The Court quoted with approval a lower court's declaration that "there is no showing that discontinuance of (the) discriminatory admission practices would inhibit in any way the teaching in these schools of any ideas or dogma."[79] This draws an implausibly sharp line between practice and ideas. If the schools are integrated, it is hard to imagine that this will not have some effect on the ideas taught.

The question of a right to exclude based on free speech was taken up again in 1984, this time much more sympathetically, in *Roberts v. United States Jaycees.*[80] In *Roberts,* the Court held that a state could constitutionally require an all-male association of young businessmen to admit women as full voting members, where previously they had been admitted only as nonvoting participants. The Court's opinion reaffirmed the proposition that the freedom of speech that the First Amendment guarantees is often exercised collectively and so entails a certain degree of freedom of association. That liberty, in turn, sometimes entails a right to exclude unwanted members:

> There can be no clearer example of an intrusion into the internal structure or affairs of an association than a regulation that forces the group to accept members it does not desire. Such a regulation may impair the ability of the original members to express only those views that brought them together. Freedom of association therefore plainly presupposes a freedom not to associate.[81]

At the same time that it embraced this more expansive view of the type of interference that might give rise to a First Amendment claim, the Court also imposed doctrinal limits upon the right it had thus created. First and foremost, it demanded the factual showing that had been implicitly deemed unnecessary in *NAACP v. Alabama*. While interference with membership "*may* impair" the association's expressive activities,[82] the association must establish the nature of its expressive practice and demonstrate just how changes in its membership will undermine that practice. The Jaycees failed in its claim, in part, because of its inability to make a sufficient showing on that score.[83] (One can easily imagine a case going the other way: the Ku Klux Klan could show that its message required the exclusion of blacks, Catholics, and Jews, for instance.)[84]

In addition, the Court held that even interference with membership that demonstrably interferes with expressive practice could be justified by "compelling state interests, unrelated to the suppression of ideas, that cannot be achieved through means significantly less restrictive of associational freedoms."[85] The result was a balancing test: antidiscrimination norms could legitimately be imposed on associations in the absence of a convincing showing of expressive burden, and perhaps even where such a burden exists, if the state interest is great enough. In practice, free association claims unrelated to viewpoint discrimination always lost in the Supreme Court under this standard.[86]

The successful association claims in the Supreme Court were brought by political parties, the expressive nature of which was indisputable. The Court invalidated state restrictions on political parties' control over their primaries, for example.[87] In earlier cases, the Court also limited the ability of states to punish individuals for belonging to groups that engaged in unlawful activities or advocated the violent overthrow of the government.[88]

Was the *Roberts* approach the correct one? Does it make sense for a right to discriminate to be rooted in the First Amendment?

The First Amendment does not speak of freedom of association. It does include "the right of the people peaceably to assemble, and to petition the government for a redress of grievances." But this has always been understood to mean a right to hold public meetings, not to exclude people from associations.[89]

More pertinently, the amendment says that Congress (and, through the Civil War amendments, the states as well) "shall make no law abridging the freedom of speech." The amendment's language is broad, but no one reads the protection of free speech literally, as protecting all uses of language, since this would invalidate much of the law of crimes, contracts, evidence, commercial transactions, antitrust, and securities, all of which in various ways restrict the use of language.

Rather, courts have held that speech is specially protected only when law regulating it in some way offends the concerns that are the reasons for protecting speech. These reasons are familiar. The people can't control the government if the government gets to control what the people think.[90] Discussion controlled by the state is less likely to discover truth than a free market of ideas.[91] Human dignity depends on the freedom of the mind.[92]

Each of these is implicated, under some circumstances, by laws that interfere with the freedom of association. For example, if the purpose of free speech is to enable people to criticize incumbent officeholders, then restrictions on association may impair that purpose. Government may try to regulate associations for the purpose of preventing opponents of incumbent officeholders from organizing to vote the officeholders out. This was precisely what was happening in *NAACP v. Alabama*.

A second reason for free speech is to promote a competition among ideas, not only with respect to expressly political matters, but about the entire spectrum of matters of public discourse. Here, too, association is valuable. The basic argument is stated by the *Roberts* Court:

> An individual's freedom to speak, to worship, and to petition the government for the redress of grievances could not be vigorously protected from interference by the State unless a correlative freedom to engage in group effort toward those ends were not also guaranteed. According protection to collective effort on behalf of shared goals is especially important in preserving political and cultural diversity and in shielding dissident expression from suppression by the majority.[93]

When this reasoning is applied to groups, the free speech concern merges into a more general concern about the importance of a civil society uncontrolled by the state. Political theorists have for decades elaborated on the functions of an unregulated civil society in a democracy. Associations are a center of collective political resistance against an oppressive government. They organize people for democratic participation, whether or not they are overtly political in their purpose. They socialize people into the political values that are necessary for self-government.[94]

The freedom of the mind rationale for speech protection is implicated when people are forced into associations they do not want. The kind of manipulation they are subjected to is not as severe as if their access to ideas is restricted, but the objection is similar. The intrusion on individual dignity is particularly acute if the association is a highly

personal one. *Roberts* thus held that relationships were constitutionally protected when they "are distinguished by such attributes as relative smallness, a high degree of selectivity in decisions to begin and
maintain the affiliation, and seclusion from others in critical aspects of
the relationship."[95] There is thus a right of intimate association that is
distinct from the right of expressive association.

These rationales can support a right to exclude. Political associations must have the ability to exclude those who would change the
association's message. If a regulation prevents an association from
conveying its message, then dissent can be stifled, the pluralism of
civil society can be constricted, and the ability of people to create
meaningful associations for themselves is likewise cramped. Intimate
associations have even broader discretion. The dignity rationale in
Roberts would explain why there could not be a law prohibiting discrimination in the choice of marriage partner, for example.

But these same rationales support limiting the right to exclude. A
central basis for free speech is democratic legitimation. But, as we
saw, racial discrimination was used in the White Primary cases to
undermine democracy by denying black citizens any effective voting
power. Racial discrimination also subverted the functions of civil society. Black citizens were denied any power to resist government
abuses, of which there were a great many. Such discrimination made
it difficult for them to organize politically. And the customs that the
discrimination helped to maintain produced a destructive, undemo-
cratic socialization in both whites and blacks. The discriminatory labor unions in *Corsi* and *Steele* were not socializing anyone very well.

Roberts tried to balance these concerns, creating a very limited
exemption from antidiscrimination laws. There is, however, a problem with the *Roberts* approach to the question of expressive burden,
and it became apparent in *Boy Scouts of America v. Dale*. The BSA

argued that admission of gay people would impair its message. The New Jersey Supreme Court held, and Justice John Paul Stevens's dissent in the Supreme Court agreed, that the BSA had not taken any public position concerning the morality of homosexuality. But it is unseemly, and potentially abusive, for courts to tell organizations — particularly organizations with dissenting political views — what their positions are.

One can see the difficulty already in *Roberts*. The Court there held that the imposition of a nondiscrimination requirement on the Jaycees "requires no change in the Jaycees' creed of promoting the interests of young men."[96] But, of course, if the Jaycees is compelled to admit women, then "promoting the interests of young men" is likely to recede as a central creed of the organization. The Court's obliviousness to the obvious burden the antidiscrimination law imposed is not reassuring about future applications of the *Roberts* rule.

These worries appear to have played a role in encouraging the Court in *Dale* to attempt a fresh start in shaping the law of freedom of association. But the Court's efforts went horribly wrong, producing a cure for the problem that is much worse than the disease.

Signs of the Times

The Dale *Opinion*

All antidiscrimination laws are unconstitutional in all their applications.

Citizens are allowed to disobey laws whenever obedience would be perceived as endorsing some message.

Both of these propositions are absurd. However, the Supreme Court's opinion in *Boy Scouts of America v. Dale*[1] stands for at least one of them, and perhaps both. The Court's disastrous opinion offers a useful cautionary lesson in First Amendment jurisprudence: determinations of what is protected speech cannot defer either to individual speakers or to the culture as a whole, because such deference produces bizarre results.

The *Dale* Decision

James Dale joined the BSA when he was eight years old. When he turned eighteen, his membership automatically expired, but he remained in the organization as an assistant Scoutmaster. In college, he came out as gay and joined the school's lesbian and gay organization. After a picture of him appeared in the local newspaper in a story about a gay youth workshop, the BSA expelled him from the organization. The letter did not explain the reason for the expulsion. When Dale wrote to inquire why, he was told that the BSA "specifically forbid[s] membership to homosexuals."[2] Dale sued the BSA under New Jersey's antidiscrimination law. He prevailed in the New Jersey Supreme Court but ultimately lost in the U.S. Supreme Court.

The New Jersey court held that the BSA was a "public accommodation" under the statute. The BSA claimed that the application of the law to the organization would violate its freedom of expression, but the Court was "not persuaded . . . that a shared goal of Boy Scout members is to associate in order to preserve the view that homosexuality is immoral."[3] The Court noted that the BSA had not, in its public materials, taken any position whatsoever concerning the morality of homosexuality. It therefore held "that Dale's membership does not violate the Boy Scouts' right of expressive association because his inclusion would not 'affect in any significant way [the BSA's] existing members' ability to carry out their various purposes.' "[4]

The U.S. Supreme Court reversed. It reasoned as follows: (1) The BSA is an association that "engages in expressive activity" protected by the First Amendment.[5] (2) Forced inclusion of a member therefore violates the First Amendment if it "would significantly affect the Boy Scouts' ability to advocate public or private viewpoints."[6] (3) The BSA asserts that homosexual conduct is inconsistent with the values embodied in the Scout Oath and Law, particularly those represented by the requirement that Scouts be "morally straight" and "clean." (4) The Court must give deference to an organization's assertions regarding the nature of its expression. (5) "[W]e must also give deference to an association's view of what would impair its expression."[7] (6) "Dale's presence in the Boy Scouts would, at the very least, force the organization to send a message, both to the youth members and the world, that the Boy Scouts accepts homosexual conduct as a legitimate form of behavior."[8]

The opinion in *Dale* does not state a clear rule to guide lower courts, but it implies either that all antidiscrimination laws are unconstitutional in all their applications, or that citizens are allowed to disobey laws whenever obedience would be perceived as endorsing some message. The first rule is supported by propositions (1) through (5), which together permit any defendant, in litigation, to allege a message to which courts must defer. The second rule is supported by proposition (6), together with the Court's invocation of the rule against compelled speech.

Expressive Association

The new expressive association right declared by the Court has far-reaching implications. Almost any association is eligible for the protection from antidiscrimination laws that the Court provides. The decision indicates that "[a]n association must merely engage in expressive activity that could be impaired in order to be entitled to protection."[9] As Richard Epstein notes, businesses are constantly engaged in expressive activity, and so the logic of *Dale* applies to them as well as to noneconomic entities.[10] It is hard to imagine an association that is *not* expressive under *Dale*'s criteria.

Once an entity is found to be entitled to protection, the only remaining question is whether the law impairs its expression. *Dale* indicates that the court must never interrogate the stated purposes of any association, and must defer to the association's view of what would impair its expression. It follows that an expressive association claim is available to any entity that wants to discriminate at any time for any purpose.

The Court's remarkable degree of deference is well illustrated by the facts of *Dale*. The BSA had no express policy about homosexuality, and its stated position was and is that "boys should learn about sex and family life from their parents, consistent with their spiritual beliefs."[11] Until the BSA started kicking out gays, many members did not know that the organization had an antigay message. Dale himself had no idea that the policy existed until he was notified of his expulsion.

The Court correctly observes that "it is not the role of the courts to reject a group's expressed values because they disagree with those values or find them internally inconsistent."[12] The fact that the BSA had no apparent position on homosexuality yesterday should not preclude the organization from taking such a position today. But doesn't that mean that any entity can make a similar claim when discrimination is alleged against it? Can't any entity claim what the BSA is claiming, that the very act of discrimination shows an expressive purpose?

Consider the following hypothetical. Ollie's Barbecue was a restaurant notorious in some quarters for the time, some decades ago, when it litigated its right to exclude blacks, all the way to the Supreme Court.[13] Suppose it were still open,[14] and that tomorrow it decides that it expresses a message of white supremacy and segregation. It therefore claims a right to exclude blacks, since including them would burden the expression of its viewpoint of white supremacy.

Unlike the BSA, Ollie's is a commercial establishment. However, the BSA's noncommercial character played no role in the *Dale* opinion.[15] Commercial speech is entitled to a diminished level of First Amendment protection, but the speech at issue here is not an attempt to solicit a commercial transaction. Rather, it is entitled to the highest level of protection, and Ollie's commercial character doesn't change this. If the restaurant took out a racist ad in the paper or displayed a racist billboard, these would be protected by the First Amendment. You may be tempted to doubt that Ollie's really does express a message of white supremacy, but under *Dale* you are not permitted to doubt that; you must give deference to Ollie's assertions regarding the nature of its expression. You must also give deference to Ollie's view of what would impair its expression. These requirements of deference are not just procedural provisos that shift the burden of establishing certain facts. They tilt the balance so radically as to transform the underlying law. It is as if there were a new rule of procedure in murder cases, holding that the court must always defer to the defendant's claims of self-defense. The presumption makes the defense so strong that there is no case in which it cannot be invoked, and the underlying prohibition is thereby nullified.

This is why Justice Stevens worried that, under the majority's test, "the right of free speech effectively becomes a limitless right to exclude for every organization, whether or not it engages in any expressive activities."[16] Justice David Souter argued that the Court has made the right of expressive association into "an easy trump of any antidiscrimination law."[17]

Chief Justice Rehnquist's majority opinion denies that a group "can erect a shield against antidiscrimination laws simply by asserting that mere acceptance of a member from a particular group would impair its message."[18] But he does not explain why the logic of his opinion does not lead to that conclusion. If there is a stopping point, the court does not say where it is located.

Rehnquist, as noted in Chapter 1, was an early opponent of the Civil Rights Act of 1964. When it was being considered, he advised his friend, Senator Barry Goldwater, that the bill was unconstitutional.[19] He must have known that he could not go that far in *Dale,* and even those who are most eager to have the Court take that step hesitate to say that he did.[20] But that is where the logic of the opinion leads.

What is clear is that *Dale* is a substantial departure from the *Roberts* rule (see Chapter 1). So what rule was the Court applying? One possibility is the approach suggested by Justice Sandra Day O'Connor's concurrence in *Roberts,* which argued that the crucial distinction was that between commercial and noncommercial organizations. O'Connor thought that "an association engaged exclusively in protected expression enjoys First Amendment protection of both the content of its message and the choice of its members," while "there is only minimal constitutional protection of the freedom of *commercial* association."[21] She would characterize an association as commercial "when, and only when, the association's activities are not predominantly of the type protected by the First Amendment."[22] She gave the BSA as an example of the importance of context: "Even the training of outdoor survival skills or participation in community service might become expressive when the activity is intended to develop good morals, reverence, patriotism, and a desire for self-improvement."[23] The Court did not state O'Connor's limiting principle in its opinion, but she provided the majority's fifth vote and there is no reason to think that she had changed her mind since *Roberts.*[24] On the other hand, the Court's opinion stressed the expressive (rather than the noncommercial) nature of the BSA. Daniel Farber observes that "the commercial or noncommercial character of an enterprise is only a rough proxy for its expressive nature."[25] O'Connor did not write separately in *Dale,* and it is premature to say that the commercial/ noncommercial distinction made in her *Roberts* concurrence of sixteen years earlier — a distinction that is not even mentioned in the *Dale* opinion — is now the law of the land.[26]

All we can say for certain, then, is that the Court cannot mean what it has said about the scope of freedom of association. Rehnquist understood that he was not going to get what he had tried to get in 1964. The fears of Stevens and Souter are therefore probably misplaced. But we have left the text of the *Dale* opinion behind.[27]

There is another argument in *Dale* that offers a different rule of law, based on the law of compelled speech.

Compelled Symbolic Speech

If one focuses on the Court's declaration that Dale's mere presence as a member of the BSA would convey a message that the BSA may not be required to convey, then most of the opinion's reasoning drops away as surplusage.[28] To compel the BSA to admit Dale, the Court held, "would, at the very least, force the organization to send a message, both to the youth members and the world, that the Boy Scouts accepts homosexual conduct as a legitimate form of behavior."[29] The case, the Court reasoned, was analogous to *Hurley v. Irish-American Gay, Lesbian and Bisexual Group of Boston, Inc.*,[30] which held that the organizers of a private St. Patrick's Day parade could not be required to include a group bearing a banner identifying itself as the Irish-American Gay, Lesbian and Bisexual Group of Boston (GLIB). "As the presence of GLIB in Boston's St. Patrick's Day parade would have interfered with the parade organizers' choice not to propound a particular point of view, the presence of Dale as an assistant scoutmaster would just as surely interfere with the Boy Scouts' choice not to propound a point of view contrary to its beliefs."[31]

The First Amendment, it is well settled, protects the right not to speak. The Court has dismissed the idea "that a Bill of Rights which guards the individual's right to speak his own mind, left it open to public authorities to compel him to utter what is not in his mind."[32] People may not be required "to repeat an objectionable message out of their own mouths" or "to use their own property to convey an antagonistic ideological message."[33] This right is not contingent on any finding that the message being sent is antagonistic to the speaker's own views. The fact that the speaker objects is sufficient.[34] Thus, propositions (1) through (5) in the Court's reasoning, outlined above, are irrelevant to the compelled speech argument.

Why did the Court think that inclusion of Dale as a member of the BSA would amount to compelled speech? The answer cannot be deference to the views of the person objecting to the law. The forced association argument considered above has radical implications, but they are confined to antidiscrimination law. If, on the other hand, one is excused from obeying *any* law if obedience would send a message, and the objector gets to decide whether obedience sends a message, then all laws are invalid in all their applications because this defense will be available in a prosecution for any violation of the law, from double parking to homicide. The Court, we may presume, did not want to constitutionalize anarchism.

To understand the compelled speech holding, it is necessary to closely parse the paragraph in which the *Dale* Court disavows the apparently destructive effects of its holding:

> We must then determine whether Dale's presence as an assis-
> tant scoutmaster would significantly burden the Boy Scouts'
> desire to not "promote homosexual conduct as a legitimate
> form of behavior." As we give deference to an association's as-
> sertions regarding the nature of its expression, we must also

give deference to an association's view of what would impair its expression. That is not to say that an expressive association can erect a shield against antidiscrimination laws simply by asserting that mere acceptance of a member from a particular group would impair its message. But here Dale, by his own admission, is one of a group of gay Scouts who have "become leaders in their community and are open and honest about their sexual orientation." Dale was the copresident of a gay and lesbian organization at college and remains a gay rights activist. Dale's presence in the Boy Scouts would, at the very least, force the organization to send a message, both to the youth members and the world, that the Boy Scouts accepts homosexual conduct as a legitimate form of behavior.[35]

The first sentence is somewhat ambiguous as to whether the issue is one of impaired freedom of association or of compelled speech. The second sentence announces deference with respect to the question raised by *Roberts,* whether forced association impairs a group's ability to send its own message. The third sentence then states that this is not a blanket nullification of all antidiscrimination laws. The next sentence, by beginning with "But . . . ," indicates that it will isolate the aspect of Dale's own case that entitled the BSA to prevail in the instant case.

What was peculiar about James Dale? The next two sentences identify specific facts about him that distinguish him as "a gay rights activist." Evidently it is because of these facts that associating with him would "force the organization to send a message."[36] How important is it that he was, not merely openly gay, but an "activist"? Evidently not very, since the Court's reasoning presupposes a remarkably capacious interpretation of what can make one an "activist." The relevant passage from the news article that was the basis of Dale's expulsion reads:

> James Dale, 19, co-president of the Rutgers University Lesbian Gay Alliance with Sharice Richardson, also 19, said he lived a double life while in high school, pretending to be straight while attending a military academy.
>
> He remembers dating girls and even laughing at homophobic jokes while at school, only admitting his homosexuality during his second year at Rutgers.
>
> "I was looking for a role model, someone who was gay and accepting of me," Dale said, adding he wasn't just seeking sexual experiences, but a community that would take him in and provide him with a support network and friends.[37]

If these three paragraphs buried inside a minor news story forever brand Dale as an "activist," then the only way a gay man can avoid being an "activist" is to remain deeply closeted.[38]

The Court's opinion puts its imprimatur on the idea that Dale's presence itself is a message. The Court holds that anyone who associates with him is therefore propounding a point of view. It evidently agrees with the claim in the BSA's brief that the exclusion of openly gay people was the only way that the BSA could *avoid* taking a public position on the morality of homosexual conduct.[39] Arthur Leonard's summary of the case's holding is not unfair: "An openly gay man so constantly and inescapably broadcasts a message about the moral and social acceptability of homosexuality that an organization that does not want to broadcast such a message is entitled to deny him membership."[40]

This interpretation of the social meaning of Dale's inclusion is unpleasant, but it may be accurate. If the Court's task is to determine whether speech is being compelled, then such interpretations are an unavoidable part of the Court's business. If people cannot be required to transmit messages, then the Court must determine what is and is not a message. One illustration is *Wooley v. Maynard*,[41] in which a Jehovah's Witness objected on religious and political grounds to the requirement that New Hampshire license plates bear the motto "Live Free or Die." When he was prosecuted for attempting to cover up the motto, the Supreme Court framed the issue as "whether the State may constitutionally require an individual to participate in the dissemination of an ideological message by displaying it on his private property in a manner and for the express purpose that it be observed and read by the public."[42] Overturning the conviction, the Court declared that the law made him into an "instrument," a "mobile billboard"[43], a "courier"[44] for a "point of view," an "ideological message," or an "idea [he] find[s] morally objectionable."[45] But as James Madigan notes, this holding necessarily has limits:

> Presumably the plaintiff in *Wooley* would have no case if he objected to the words "New Hampshire," and at most an extremely weak case if the plate read "My car is registered in New Hampshire." One doubts that the person who resides and drives in New Hampshire will be able to escape carrying the state name simply because she hates her state. *Wooley* never suggests that the license plates themselves or their non-ideological numerals and letters could be challenged.[46]

Madigan concludes that the *Dale* decision is erroneous because Dale himself did not express any message. If his very presence was taken to convey a message, "[t]he content of that message is nothing more than the Boy Scouts' characterization; after all, James Dale said nothing in the context of Scouting about being gay, and he said nothing in the context of gay activities about being a Scoutmaster."[47] The Court, however, did not leave the BSA free to attribute any message it liked to Dale's presence. Rather, the Court determined, as a matter of law, what Dale's presence meant. In the context of an inherently expressive event like the parade in *Hurley,* this conclusion might be less controversial. In the context of a prosaic association of people engaged in a myriad of activities that are not inherently expressive — like camping[48] — it requires closer interrogation.

The soundness of the Court's conclusion depends on whether it correctly interpreted the meaning of Dale's inclusion. This is a question, not of law, but of cultural anthropology. The semantic meaning of behavior is always a function of the conventions that obtain at a particular time and place.[49] Depending on what conventions happen to exist, a person's inclusion may well be speech. The day the Supreme Court ruled against him, James Dale declared in an interview: "I'm not a message. I'm not a symbol. I'm not a sign. I'm just a person who happens to be gay."[50] But this is a false dichotomy. Depending on the cultural background, *anything* can be a sign.

Steven D. Smith observes that perceptions of what behavior constitutes endorsement are parasitic on one's background norms of appropriate, neutral behavior. Thus, for example, it is widely thought that the establishment clause prohibits the state from supporting religion, but no one thinks that this is what is happening when the church is burning and the fire department puts it out. This is not endorsement. It is just what fire departments do. On the other hand, the state would certainly be sending a symbolic message if the firefighters stood by and watched the church burn.[51]

The question of whether the BSA has "endorsed" homosexual conduct, then, depends on one's background assumptions about what sort of action is normally appropriate. If one is behaving appropriately, then one is behaving neutrally and avoiding improper favoritism.[52] The idea of "endorsement" is always parasitic in this way. Following the unspoken norm endorses nothing; only departing from the norm sends a message.[53] It follows that, depending on what the unspoken norm happens to be, the imperative of avoiding symbolic endorsement can justify anything.[54]

The decision to voluntarily and publicly associate with a pariah has conventional meaning because it so openly defies a conventional norm. Baseball teams aren't now understood to be making a statement when they add well-qualified players to their rosters — that's just what baseball teams do — but the Brooklyn Dodgers necessarily and inevitably made a statement when it decided to hire Jackie Robinson in 1947.

If it is assumed that gay people normally have pariah status, that they are inherently predatory and unclean, then ostracism is the normal, neutral response to this condition. It does not send a message, any more than a fire department does when it extinguishes a fire in a church.

The inclusion of gay people in ordinary pursuits remains controversial. And that is why, whenever someone refuses to discriminate against gays, that person is often perceived as making a statement of approval of homosexual conduct. The Court was not idiosyncratic in its perception of the conventional meaning of Dale's inclusion.

Law routinely incorporates conventional meanings into its determinations. If it did not, it is not clear how it could distinguish "Live Free or Die" from the number on a license plate. But there must be limits on such reliance. In *Plessy v. Ferguson*,[55] the Court upheld a law requiring racial segregation by reasoning that the legislature was at "liberty to act with reference to the established usages, customs, and traditions of the people."[56] Numerous cases from the Jim Crow South held, on the basis of those established usages and customs, that calling a white person black was an actionable humiliation.[57]

Conventions change over time, of course. And semantic meanings change as conventions change. No message is perceived now when a restaurant like Ollie's Barbecue seats black customers. The situation the day after the restaurant lost its case, however, was very different. It is only when the law is trying to change established social practice that the required conduct will be reasonably understood as sending a message.

It follows that, if the compelled speech doctrine is understood in the way the *Dale* Court understands it, the First Amendment will preclude law from operating in those areas where convention is most resistant. Prejudices will be insulated from the law precisely to the extent that they are widespread. Here we see a contemporary analogue of the pariah assumption that, we saw in Chapter 1, contaminated the earliest formulations of freedom of association: some kinds of discrimination are especially privileged in the law because there are some people with whom no reasonable person would want to associate. *Dale* thus stands on its head the holding of *Palmore v. Sidoti*[58] that "[p]rivate biases may be outside the reach of the law, but the law cannot, directly or indirectly, give them effect."[59] *Dale* implicitly holds that the Court has a duty to discern the private biases that exist and to give them effect by making them the basis for exemptions from generally applicable laws. Prejudice is thereby given a legal privilege that is denied to religious scruples.[60] This is, of course, entirely at odds with the settled understanding of the Fourteenth Amendment, which precludes government from imposing badges of inferiority.[61] The Court's ratification of popular prejudices has its own symbolic meaning, and it is not pretty.[62]

Thus, like the expressive association claim, the compelled speech claim, as stated by the *Dale* Court, reaches farther than the Court could possibly have intended. The compelled speech argument has implications that are even more destructive than the expressive association argument, which would have invalidated only antidiscrimination laws.

The compelled speech claim would invalidate any law that requires conduct that can reasonably be understood as having symbolic meaning. Federal regulations now require cars to have airbags. These regulations were adopted despite the resistance of automobile manufacturers. When new cars conspicuously have airbags, this is reasonably understood as sending a message that (1) airbags are necessary to make cars safe and that (2) their inclusion is cost-justified—both propositions from which the manufacturer may dissent. Under *Dale,* does the manufacturer not have a powerful argument that its First Amendment rights are being violated by compelled speech?[63]

Once more, the rule stated by the Court is absurdly broad unless it is supplemented by a limiting principle that appears nowhere in the opinion. The crucial and unprecedented move is *Dale*'s extension of the compelled speech doctrine to include symbolic speech. Because any kind of conduct can convey a message, the Court has been unwilling to say that all communicative conduct is protected by the First Amendment. When a person *refuses* to obey a law because he or she wishes to engage in symbolic conduct—say, burning a draft card or violating a curfew in a public park to protest homelessness—the law may nonetheless be applied to that person "if it is within the constitutional power of the Government; if it furthers an important or substantial governmental interest; if the governmental interest is unrelated to the suppression of free expression; and if the incidental restriction on alleged First Amendment freedoms is no greater than is essential to the furtherance of that interest."[64] In practice, this test has been very deferential; "the Court virtually never invalidates a regulation once it has found it to be content neutral."[65]

The anarchic potential of *Dale*'s compelled speech rationale dwarfs that of the symbolic conduct cases. The compelled speech doctrine is absolute and does not permit balancing. The symbolic conduct cases involved parties who wanted to disobey a law to send a message, and their claim rested on their unusual attempt to convey their message by their conduct. *Dale*'s rationale, however, does not find speech in disobedience, but in obedience, so that once a law is found to compel symbolic conduct, *anyone* is authorized to resist it — not only those who are affirmatively trying to convey a message.

The Ominous Context

There are two other contemporaneous bits of evidence that the *Dale* Court expanded the freedom of association beyond all reasonable bounds. One is its decision in a compelled speech case which suggested that all of corporate law might be subject to First Amendment scrutiny. The other is an election law case which suggests that the Court is entirely blind to countervailing interests. The Court held that the desire of the voters of a state to be able to democratically select their leaders has no weight against a political party's internal freedom of association.

In a series of cases involving compelled commercial speech, the Court suggested that any organization that engages in commercial speech is an expressive association and that a requirement to affiliate with such an organization implicates First Amendment rights.[66] Such a rule, Robert Post observes, "threatens to constitutionalize much of the law of corporations and business organizations."[67] Virtually all business organizations engage in commercial speech, and the law of association forces people to associate with one another in a broad range of business contexts. The Court cannot mean to imply that all of corporate law is presumptively unconstitutional. These tendencies in the case law suggest that the Court is endorsing a broad right of association without much reflection.

What about the state interests at stake in these association cases? *Roberts v. United States Jaycees* held that even regulation of membership that demonstrably interferes with expressive practice could be justified by "compelling state interests, unrelated to the suppression of ideas, that cannot be achieved through means significantly less restrictive of associational freedoms."[68] The Supreme Court's opinion in *Dale* declares that "[t]he state interests embodied in New Jersey's public accommodations law do not justify such a severe intrusion on the Boy Scouts' rights to freedom of association,"[69] but, remarkably, it never says what these interests are.

The Court's narrow conception of state interests was made clear in *California Democratic Party v. Jones,*[70] decided two days before *Dale.*[71] *Jones* struck down a California law that mandated blanket primaries, in which voters could vote for any candidate regardless of the voter's party affiliation. The Court, in an opinion by Justice Antonin Scalia, held that the law violated political parties' freedom of association. Parties have a right to select their nominees without interference from outsiders.

California defended its rule by claiming that blanket primaries tended to produce more moderate nominees, whose views were more reflective of the views of the majority of voters than those selected by party regulars. The Court held that this was not only not a compelling reason to interfere with the party's internal autonomy; it was not even a *permissible* government interest. The goal of "producing elected officials who better represent the electorate," Justice Scalia declared, was "simply circumlocution for producing nominees and nominee positions other than those the parties would choose if left to their own devices." This interest was "nothing more than a stark repudiation of freedom of political association: Parties should not be free to select their own nominees because those nominees, and the positions taken by those nominees, will not be congenial to the majority."[72]

The Court's condemnation of state interference with party autonomy, Samuel Issacharoff observes, is so sweeping that it calls into question any state regulation of political parties, even the requirement that they hold primaries at all.[73] The parties do not operate independently of the state. It is only because the electoral mechanism calls for single-member electoral districts that there are only two major parties, largely immune from displacement by third-party competitors. In declaring that the electorate has no legitimate interest in influencing the identity of party nominees, the Court comes dangerously close to declaring that it is none of the public's business who their elected officials are. It is hard to imagine a deeper obliviousness to the destructive effects of an unlimited freedom of association.

In short, *Dale* is confused about both the scope of the right and what gets balanced against the right. We need to think about how to do better. But first, we need to look at the consequences of *Dale*.

3

The Solomon Amendment Litigation and Other Consequences of *Dale*

The pathological implications of *Dale* were brought to the Court's attention in a striking way in *Rumsfeld v. FAIR*,[1] and the Court, unsurprisingly, retreated from those implications. This chapter will show how this happened. The destructive potential of *Dale* was underestimated by many in the *FAIR* litigation, notably the plaintiffs, who operated under the sincere but misplaced belief that their arguments were advancing the antidiscrimination cause.

More than any other area of constitutional law, the doctrines that govern the speech clause of the First Amendment suffer from the risk that form may come to override function. The potential ambit of free speech doctrine is huge, since most types of collective human activity necessarily involve speech, and the rise of robust constitutional protection for freedom of speech in the modern era has been accompanied by an inevitable proliferation of complex doctrines. These free speech doctrines must distinguish between expression that should enjoy protection from state interference and conduct that should not, even when the conduct in question is accomplished in part through the medium of speech. When at its best, First Amendment doctrine uses sensitive, contextual analysis to identify and protect those forms of expression that play some role in democratic self-governance, human flourishing, and the expansion of collective knowledge. When not at its best, however, the First Amendment can become a self-propelled and self-justifying juggernaut, demanding outcomes that claim to be the inevitable, algorithmic result of established free speech precedents but are in fact profoundly disconnected from the underlying reality and the animating values to which they purport to give voice.

The series of lawsuits that sought to challenge the constitutionality of the federal Solomon Amendment under the First Amendment doctrine of "expressive association" fell decisively into the latter category. The Solomon Amendment requires that universities afford equal and unfettered access to military recruiters during the on-campus interview process, despite the military's discriminatory behavior toward gay recruits — behavior that would otherwise call for the recruiters to be excluded from portions of the recruitment process under the nondiscrimination policies of many institutions. Born of a well-intentioned effort to express tangible support for the gay, lesbian, and bisexual students who are excluded by the military's "Don't Ask, Don't Tell" policy, these lawsuits threatened to bring about a crisis in the doctrine of expressive association. This potential crisis became acute when the law professor plaintiffs secured a pair of victorious opinions from federal courts in the U.S. Court of Appeals for the Third Circuit[2] and the District of Connecticut[3] that had appalling implications for the enforceability of other important laws and progressive reforms. Ultimately, the Supreme Court defused the situation by reversing the Third Circuit and upholding the constitutionality of the Solomon Amendment in a unanimous opinion that was more an exercise in damage control than in analytical cogency.

The doctrinal crisis provoked by the Solomon litigation offers a picture in microcosm of the current state of expressive association and the crossroads at which this doctrine stands.

Military Recruitment and the Solomon Amendment

One of the earliest victories of the gay rights movement came when some institutions in mainstream America embraced the view that discrimination against gay people is, in at least some respects, analogous to racism. Quite early on, some elite institutions became convinced that the two kinds of discrimination were equally pernicious. For example, as early as 1978, Yale Law School extended its nondiscrimination policy (which had first been promulgated in 1972) to bar discrimination on the basis of sexual orientation.[4]

Gradually, these nondiscrimination policies spread across many law school campuses, were adopted by the Association of American Law Schools (AALS), and became the norm at accredited institutions around the country. The policies also expanded to include the activities of employers who sought to recruit law students from these institutions. In 1990, the AALS added sexual orientation to its nondiscrimination policy, requiring both public and private employers to sign a pledge that they would not discriminate against a law school's gay, lesbian, and bisexual students before the employers would be given full access to the recruitment apparatus and permitted to come on campus to conduct interviews.[5]

Such nondiscrimination policies were an unwelcome development for the military, which recruits, among many other places, on law school campuses, seeking to fill the ranks of its Judge Advocate Gen-

eral's Corps, or JAG. As an arm of the military, JAG overtly discriminates against gay, lesbian, and bisexual employees as a matter of official
military policy.[6] When law schools began to enforce their antidiscrimination policies and exclude military recruiters from the campus interview process, the Pentagon and the military grew upset with this
highly visible expression of institutional disapproval, and also with
what they claimed to be a threat to their ability to staff JAG ranks.[7]
Congress responded by enacting a law, the Solomon Amendment, that
put financial pressure on law schools to excuse the military from
complying with their antidiscrimination rules by denying certain types
of federal funding to institutions that barred military recruitment on
campus. This pressure has steadily increased and is now overwhelming
for law schools that exist as part of larger research universities.

The Solomon Amendment was first enacted in 1995 and has since
been amended several times.[8] The amendment originally was interpreted to remove federal funding only from the part of the university
that placed limitations on military recruiters. Thus, for example, if a
university's law school barred military recruiters from portions of the
hiring process, only the law school, not the entire university, would
lose funding.[9] In 1999, however, the statute was amended to bar
funding for an entire university if any part of it treated military recruiters less favorably.[10] Almost all American universities receive large
amounts of federal funds, and the prospect of losing those funds
would have been a financial disaster. So law schools gave in to this
financial pressure and allowed recruiters on campus.

Some law schools and individual law professors then sued to challenge the constitutionality of the Solomon Amendment. Two of these
cases produced constitutional rulings: *FAIR v. Rumsfeld,* a suit in-
stituted by a large array of institutions and groups of faculty members,
and *Burt v. Rumsfeld,* a suit brought solely by members of the faculty

of Yale Law School.[11] After producing a remarkably broad victory on behalf of the plaintiffs in the U.S. Court of Appeals for the Third Circuit (a victory that was subsequently echoed in the Yale Law School suit), the former suit came before the Supreme Court, styled as *Rumsfeld v. FAIR*.

The constitutional argument that the plaintiffs in these cases offered was based on the First Amendment. They made two claims. First, they argued that, by enacting their antidiscrimination policies, law schools were communicating a message: "Discrimination against gay men and lesbians is wrong and will not be tolerated." By forcing them to allow recruiters on campus who discriminate against gay students, the professors and law schools argued, Solomon impeded their ability to communicate or exemplify this inclusive message. Second, they argued that the military had its own message that it conveys when it recruits: "Discrimination against gay men and lesbians is acceptable and necessary for the military mission." Law schools argued that, by forcing them to facilitate the dissemination of this message, the Solomon Amendment was compelling them to say things with which they disagreed.

Both First Amendment arguments depended heavily upon expansive interpretations of *Boy Scouts of America v. Dale*. The plaintiffs in *Rumsfeld v. FAIR* argued that their position was exactly the same as that of the BSA and that the expansive doctrines of the *Dale* case should apply with equal force to the claims of any association that asserts that it has an expressive mission.

Equality and Speech in the Law of Expressive Association

To appreciate the doctrinal crisis that the Solomon litigation provoked, it is necessary to understand the manner in which the Solomon plaintiffs proposed to amplify the shift that the *Dale* decision had effectuated in the law of expressive association. This understanding must operate on both a doctrinal and a conceptual level. On the level of doctrine, the Solomon plaintiffs embraced a ruling that vastly expanded expressive association rights in one particular context — an organization, the BSA, that was engaged in quintessentially noncommercial activity, operated predominantly in small and local groups, and faced a challenge to control over its membership and leadership positions — and sought to explode that context, asking for these expanded rights to apply to enormous and powerful quasi-corporate institutions that were elaborately involved in commerce and were under no threat to their control over membership. On a conceptual level, the Solomon plaintiffs sought to entrench and expand the signature move of the *Dale* opinion: the framing of expressive association claims exclusively in terms of speech values, rather than as a composite of speech and equality principles, the frame employed by *Dale*'s predecessors. In both respects, the litigation sought to push the law of expressive association in unsustainable directions.

The decision in *Dale* represented an enormous departure from its predecessors. Despite a litigation context that appeared to be a natural progression from *Roberts v. United States Jaycees* and its progeny, the *Dale* majority, as explained at length in Chapter 2, shifted to an extraordinarily permissive standard in the factual showing that it demanded of associational claimants. The Court adopted a posture of almost complete deference to an association's claim that an antidiscrimination law's interference with decisions about a small number of members would undermine the group's expressive practice. Yet the Court also indicated that its decision did not create an unlimited right to discriminate, leaving confusion about just what its holding was.

Cases after *Dale* revealed the unsustainably broad implications of the

Court's opinion, along with lower courts' reluctance to follow out those implications. Courts have rejected numerous *Dale*-based claims.[12] In so doing, they have consistently found it necessary to confine *Dale*'s reach on the basis of distinctions that either do not appear in the opinion or which the opinion uses in a far broader way than the lower courts were willing to do. The logic of the *Dale* opinion made the claimants' arguments colorable in all these cases, but the lower courts were unwilling to follow that opinion's logic to its conclusions.

In some cases, the courts declared that conduct that obviously had expressive dimensions was nonetheless not expressive.[13] Another response was to hold that conduct which could be taken by third parties to convey a message was nonetheless not expressive.[14] A few decisions held that *Dale* was concerned only with membership, so that burdens on association which did not compel membership did not run afoul of *Dale*.[15]

One notably weak distinction was drawn in a case involving a statute banning children's access to a public clothing-optional park. The case looked a lot like *Dale;* both the nudists and the BSA were being prevented from instilling certain values in children. The court declared that the nudists, unlike the BSA, were trying to protect "not the activity itself, but rather, the manner in which the activity is conducted—in the nude and in public."[16] Of course, the *Dale* Court could as easily have said that the BSA was trying to protect the manner in which its activities were conducted—away from gay people.

The difficulty of getting out from under the broad reach of *Dale* is particularly clear in *Catholic Charities of the Diocese of Albany v. Serio*,[17] in which an organization objected to a law requiring employers that provided group prescription drug insurance coverage to include prescription contraceptives in that coverage. "Plaintiffs' contention that they are being 'grouped' in some inchoate manner with employers who provide contraceptive coverage does not demonstrate an affiliation that is sufficient to support an expressive association claim,"[18] the court declared. Nor would Catholic Charities be perceived as endorsing contraceptives:

> Given plaintiffs' well-known religious beliefs regarding contraception, we cannot conclude that there is a "great likelihood" that plaintiffs' provision of contraceptive coverage to its employees would be perceived as anything more than compliance under protest with a statutory mandate that is generally applicable to all employers offering group health insurance coverage, rather than conduct undertaken for an expressive purpose.[19]

(Of course, the same answer could have been given to the BSA in *Dale,* since it, too, would have complied under protest had it lost the case.)

The sole dissenting judge offered pointed answers to both these arguments. On the forced association claim, he noted, quoting *Dale,* that "being forced to provide a message of support for contraceptives (by paying for them), 'sends a distinctly different message' from their official position on the subject and 'significantly affect[s] its expression.'"[20] He likewise took the expressive conduct prong of *Dale* to its logical implications: the law "violates plaintiffs' free speech rights because it compels them to engage in *conduct* that communicates a message of support for contraceptive use that is in violation of their religious beliefs."[21] The rule this judge inferred from *Dale* is the same one we offered as a *reductio ad absurdum* in Chapter 2: citizens are entitled to disobey laws whenever obedience would be perceived as endorsing some message.

One court, evidently in despair at finding any basis for distinguishing *Dale,* simply ignored its reasoning. Upholding a city ordinance prohibiting discrimination on the basis of sexual orientation, the court relied entirely upon a pre-*Dale* statement by the Supreme Court that "[i]nvidious private discrimination may be characterized as a form of exercising freedom of association protected by the First Amendment, but it has never been accorded affirmative constitutional protections."[22]

Another strategy is to distort the facts of *Dale* in order to distinguish the instant case. Upholding the application of an antidiscrimination law to a fraternal order that was generally unselective about its membership but that discriminated against women, a court wrote of *Dale:* "Because the antihomosexual value was central, frequently asserted, and long-standing, and because accepting an acknowledged homosexual as a scout leader would send a message of acceptance that was contrary to that value, such acceptance would significantly interfere with the organization's ability to express its message."[23] Of course, the *Dale* Court found no such facts, and the lower court had in fact found the contrary; all the work in *Dale* was done by the court's deference to the organization, which would have produced the same result in this case or in any discrimination case.

Before the Solomon litigation, only three reported cases relied on *Dale* in upholding a claim of freedom of association.[24] The BSA itself was a party in two of these, one of which carves out a category of "nonexpressive" jobs in the Scouting organization, to which *Dale* does not apply.[25] The other involved a males-only meeting conducted by the Nation of Islam and thus raised questions of the autonomy of religious groups that are different from those presented by ordinary association claims.[26] Until the lower court decisions in the FAIR cases, no court had upheld a *Dale* claim involving a nonreligious association other than the BSA. The lower federal courts were well on their way to confining *Dale* to its facts.[27]

For all its broad language, the *Dale* decision involved a factual situation that could be understood as placing many limitations on the new doctrine that it had announced. (None of these was declared to be relevant in the *Dale* opinion, but as we saw in Chapter 2, that opinion was so poorly crafted that it stated no intelligible rule at all.) Unlike many technically not-for-profit entities, the BSA really does engage almost entirely in activities that are far removed from commerce. It is an organization of youth, largely supervised by volunteer adults, who go camping and participate in other recreational and community activities. Earlier Supreme Court decisions had made clear that the noncommercial character of an organization's pursuits would weigh in favor of an expressive association claim. Moreover, the State of New Jersey had sought to compel the BSA to accept, not just a youth member (that is, another Scout), but a person in a leadership position, placing the BSA on firmer ground in arguing that the *Roberts* decision, with its references to membership and interference with expression, supported its claim. And the BSA, though a national organization, operated on a small scale in locally organized groups, painting a sympathetic picture of an informal entity that should remain free from state regulation. The *Dale* decision was still wrong, and dangerously so, in exempting the BSA from making the factual showings about the nature of its expressive activities and the alleged interference with those activities that *Roberts* had long required. But it was still possible (and lower courts were inclined) to approach the *Dale* case as articulating a rule that would apply, if at all, in only a limited context in future cases.

The law professor plaintiffs in the Solomon litigation sought to explode that context. The expansion of *Dale* that the Solomon plaintiffs called for would have disassembled all the implicit limitations that kept that beast at bay. American law schools, unlike the BSA, are deeply and directly enmeshed with powerful commercial forces. The credentialing and regulatory rules that govern the practice of law make law schools almost the sole gatekeepers to that powerful and highly compensated profession. The activity at issue in the Solomon litigation—the manner in which law schools would manage the recruitment of their students at this high-stakes commercial job fair— was unquestionably a "commercial" activity, even if undertaken by institutions that formally operated on a not-for-profit basis. (As a point of comparison, the Jaycees also operates as a not-for-profit corporation,[28] but the Supreme Court found that it engaged in "various commercial programs" that served as important gateways to professional advancement[29] and that this "commercial nature" militated in favor of its amenability to state regulation.[30]) And law schools are powerful economic entities with clear quasi-public features: they employ large numbers of workers, collect steep tuition from students, and are presumptively open to any applicant who can qualify for admission.

What is more, the type of interference that the law schools were claiming with their expressive activities—their ability to be effective and credible in communicating a message of inclusiveness toward their gay, lesbian, and bisexual students—was a far cry from the interference that the Court had recognized in the cases stretching from *Roberts* to *Dale*. There was no question of "membership" in the Solomon litigation.[31] Solomon does not require law schools to admit anyone as a faculty member, staff employee, or student. All the law requires is that law schools permit JAG recruiters to participate on an episodic basis—typically, once or twice per year—in the job fairs that law schools host for potential employers who wish to interview their students. Presenting quite the opposite of a "membership" question, these job fairs explicitly involve the invitation of outsiders into the law school as temporary guests. The form of interference with expression that the Court recognized as a matter of principle in *Roberts,* and found as a matter of fact in *Dale,* is entirely absent on law school campuses under Solomon.

Finally, the actual core of the argument for interference with expression in the Solomon litigation was simply not credible. In plain language, the law professors claimed that their ability to express a message of inclusiveness toward their lesbian, gay, bisexual, and transgendered students was fatally undermined by the presence twice each year of JAG recruiters at the schools' commercial job fairs.[32] As FAIR put it in its main brief before the Supreme Court: "To the distress of law deans and faculty, members of their communities have concluded that the schools are not committed to antidiscrimination, and that the law schools have lost credibility to preach values of equality, justice, and human dignity."[33] One is invited to imagine that law students, upon seeing the presence of the military recruiters on campus, will either assume that the law school has invited them there as a sign of its approval of Don't Ask, Don't Tell, despite their knowledge of the law school's vigorous protests; or else that the mere presence of the recruiters at the commercial job fair "poisons the atmosphere" at a law school for the entire rest of the year, so that even students who understand that the school does not share the military's views will never again be able to hear that message from the administration or faculty with open ears.[34]

These suggestions blink reality. To be sure, faculty, staff, and students who care about these issues might be very unhappy about the presence of military recruiters and what they believe those recruiters to represent. They might even feel differently about messages of inclusiveness and equality when they must occasionally confront the discordant reality that one of our most important public institutions rejects that message. But this is not interference with the expression of law schools or law faculty. It is merely the fabric of reality against which that expression must attempt to take hold. It is no more the case that the participation of military recruiters in the law school job fairs impaired faculty expression about gay equality than it is that the requirement of paying taxes impairs expression about the philosophical belief in anarchism.

If the expansive rule of *Dale* applied, in full force, to institutions and regulations such as these, then there would truly be nothing left of the limits that *Roberts* and its progeny imposed. Any "expressive association" — which, in essence, could include almost any organization that does not pursue commercial profit as its primary activity — would have the authority to resist any form of regulation that it claimed would interfere with its ability to express its purported message.

The resulting rule would have placed in serious jeopardy the very antidiscrimination principles that the law professors sought to promote in their challenge. Under *Roberts,* it was already well established that laws affecting the ability of organizations to control their membership might sometimes infringe upon expressive rights in violation of the First Amendment. Until *Dale,* this proposition was carefully limited by the requirement of a robust factual showing and a constitutional balancing test. In *Dale,* the Court relieved the claimant of those important limitations, but it still left a good deal of room for arguing that the expansive rights it had recognized were limited to the idiosyncratic context of that particular case. Imagine, however, if the Court had granted the Solomon plaintiffs their wish and accorded all "expressive associations" the licentious deference that it gave to the BSA. What effect would such a ruling have had upon equality values?

To recap, the Solomon plaintiffs argued that an expressive association has the right to resist any form of state or federal regulation that is inconsistent with its values, undermines its credibility in communicating a message about its values to the outside world, or forces it to take actions that are inconsistent with its desire to teach by doing and thereby exemplify its values. They further argued that such claimants need offer no factual proof of the centrality of the "values" in question to their broader expressive mission, or of the interference that they claim with their credibility in the public sphere, or of the extent to which the regulation interferes with their ability to exemplify their values by acting upon them, but rather could demand that courts defer to their assertions on all these matters. Consider how these arguments might be used in other contexts:

- Title IX of the federal Education Amendments of 1972 has been the primary vehicle by which women have gained broader access to sports opportunities in the United States. Broadly speaking, the law requires universities that accept federal funds to make roughly equal facilities and resources available to their female and male students in their sports programs. Under the position urged by the Solomon plaintiffs, a university could invoke the First Amendment to resist this requirement, simply by asserting that it values more traditional forms of activity by women and wishes to encourage its students to pursue activities that reflect more traditional gender roles. Title IX would obviously undermine the ability of the university to communicate with credibility about the traditional roles of women as much as, if not more than, the Solomon plaintiffs claimed that the presence of military recruiters interfered with their message about inclusiveness. Title IX would obviously interfere with the ability of such an institution to exemplify its value concerning traditional gender roles by structuring extracurricular programs to reflect those roles, just as Solomon interferes with the law schools' ability to exemplify antidiscrimination values. If the Solomon plaintiffs had prevailed, it appears that Title IX could be resisted by any university willing to claim a different worldview.[35]

- An increasing number of states provide some form of protection to gay men and lesbians against discrimination in employment. Under the proposed rule in the Solomon litigation, however, any expressive association — including huge, multibillion-dollar organizations like elite private universities — could resist the enforcement of those laws simply by asserting a contrary worldview. If a university were willing to say that it "values" ideas of sexual morality under which homosexuality is unacceptable, then, under the rule proposed by the Solomon plaintiffs, the university could claim a First Amendment right to fire gay or lesbian faculty, or any other employee. For that matter, such an institution could exclude and expel gay and lesbian students, state law notwithstanding. After all, if the institution's values held homosexuality to be categorically unacceptable, it would surely interfere with its credibility in communicating that message, to the same degree claimed by the Solomon plaintiffs, if they were forced to allow gay people to teach, work, and study as members of their communities. Similarly, if the university cannot maintain a putatively gay-free environment, how can it "walk the walk" and exemplify its antigay values?

This same set of arguments could be deployed as easily under the Americans with Disabilities Act, or even under laws outlawing racial discrimination. The type of discrimination involved might affect a court's assessment of the state's interest in enforcing its laws. But all antidiscrimination laws would be subject to this form of First Amendment scrutiny, and—as we suggested in deliberately alarmist terms above—perhaps all such laws would be subject to a mandatory constitutional exemption for any organization willing to embrace discriminatory values as a litigation position.[36] The *Dale* decision seemingly opened the door for this catastrophic reconfiguration of the constitutional landscape. This result is one that should be resisted, not embraced.[37]

And, indeed, the Supreme Court avoided these dangers in reversing the Third Circuit, rejecting the law professors' claims and resolving the case very narrowly. "The Solomon Amendment," Chief Justice John Roberts wrote for a unanimous Court, "neither limits what law schools may say nor requires them to say anything,"[38] bringing the case outside the ambit of both expressive association and compelled speech doctrines. For the most part, the chief justice distinguished *Dale* by ignoring it. He did not even cite the decision until he took up the forced association claim, which he rejected because "the Solomon Amendment does not force a law school 'to accept members it does not desire' "[39]—perhaps limiting *Dale* (and the *Roberts* cases as well?) to actual interference with membership. Roberts did not even deign to discuss the idea that compliance with an unwelcome law imposed symbolic behavior that would compromise a speaker's credibility or constitute compelled speech—one of the central themes of *Dale*. When he addressed the compelled speech cases, he simply distinguished them with the assertion that, in those cases, the speaker's own message was directly affected because it was forced to accommodate speech.[40] Expressive conduct, the chief justice held, is not compelled speech if it is not inherently expressive, as marching in a parade or burning a flag would be.[41]

Thus, at the close of the Solomon litigation, the law of expressive association remained in flux. The Court did not expand the *Dale* decision in the dramatic manner that the law professors had sought, but neither did it impose clear and explicit limitations on *Dale*. Indeed, the one explicit gesture of limitation contained in *Rumsfeld v. FAIR*—the Court's suggestion that interference with membership lies at the heart of the *Dale* doctrine[42]—appears to keep the door open for the litany of consequences regarding the enforcement of equality values explored in the scenarios above. While apparently not in imminent danger of a fundamental restructuring, the fate of antidiscrimination laws under the *Dale* doctrine remains unclear.

A recent case threatens to broaden the right of association once more, but in an unexpected direction. *Washington State Grange v. Washington State Republican Party*[43] upheld a state's blanket primary system, under which there was first a blanket primary for all candidates of both parties, and then the top two vote-getters would advance to the general election. The challenged provision permitted each candidate to designate a "party preference," even if the named political party objected to the candidate's doing so.

The Supreme Court, in an opinion by Justice Clarence Thomas, held that there was no infringement on the parties' rights of association: "There is simply no basis to presume that a well-informed electorate will interpret a candidate's party-preference designation to mean that the candidate is the party's chosen nominee or representative or that the party associates with or approves of the candidate."[44]

The case came to the Court on a facial challenge; it was possible that the ballot would be presented in a way that would "eliminate the possibility of widespread voter confusion and with it the perceived threat to the First Amendment."[45] For example, the ballot "could include prominent disclaimers explaining that party preference reflects only the self-designation of the candidate and not an official endorsement by the party."[46] Justice Thomas distinguished *Dale* because that case turned on more than perception: "*actual* association threatened to distort the [BSA's] intended message."[47]

A concurring opinion by Chief Justice Roberts, joined by Justice Samuel Alito, went further, declaring that "if the ballot merely lists the candidates' preferred parties next to the candidates' names, or otherwise fails clearly to convey that the parties and the candidates are not necessarily associated, the . . . system would not survive a First Amendment challenge."[48] He cited *Dale* for the proposition that "whether voters *perceive* the candidate and the party to be associated is relevant to the constitutional inquiry" because in that case "accepting Dale would lead outsiders to believe the Scouts endorsed homosexual conduct."[49]

Justice Scalia, dissenting (joined by Justice Anthony Kennedy), thought that the ballot scheme's damage to First Amendment values could not be cured by a disclaimer. "When an expressive organization is compelled to associate with a person whose views the group does not accept, the organization's message is undermined; the organization is understood to embrace, or at the very least tolerate, the views of the persons linked with them."[50] He cited *Dale* as an illustration. A candidate's statement of his or her party affiliation affects the party's message. "An individual's endorsement of a party shapes the voter's view of what the party stands for, no less than the party's endorsement of an individual shapes the voter's view of what the individual stands for."[51] There is no way to avoid the tarnishment of the party's image created by that statement. "Is it enough to say on the ballot that a notorious and despised racist who says that the party is his choice does not speak with the party's approval? Surely not. His unrebutted association of that party with his views distorts the image of the party nonetheless."[52] It should not be necessary, Scalia argued, for the party to show that its image has been distorted. Rather, "we accept their own assessments of the matter. . . . In *Dale,* for example, we did not require the Boy Scouts to prove that forced acceptance of the openly homosexual scoutmaster would distort their message."[53]

What is remarkable about all of these opinions is that they presume that the constitutional freedom of association is implicated when *the organization in question is not being regulated at all* — not being required to accept unwanted members, not being required even to be in the same building with people it finds unacceptable, not being compelled or forbidden to speak, or to do or refrain from doing anything else. The infringement on the organization's First Amendment rights consists in the fact that the state is enabling third parties to appropriate the organization's name. The Court evidently thinks that the First Amendment requires something like the constitutionalization of trademark law.[54] We are not aware of any other context in which a law that does not regulate a person at all can nonetheless be claimed to violate that person's First Amendment rights.

The *Washington State Grange* case could mean any of several things. It could be understood as a further expansion of the compelled speech holding of *Dale:* there is compelled speech, not only when someone is required to engage in conduct that will be thought by others to express a message, but when the state itself engages in conduct that causes others to think that some person is sending a message. It could, on the other hand, be applicable only in the special context of elections and concern only the right of parties to limit their endorsement of candidates. It is too soon to tell. The scope of the *Dale* right remains deeply uncertain.

4

The Neolibertarian Proposal

So the Supreme Court has gone wrong in its approach to freedom of association, and the law is in disarray. What ought the law to look like, then?

A prominent group of scholars, whom I will refer to as "neolibertarians," argue that noncommercial private associations should be given an absolute right to discriminate. (The restriction of the right to noncommercial associations is what makes them "neo.") The group is a distinguished one, including Judge Michael McConnell and professors David Bernstein, Dale Carpenter, Richard Epstein, John McGinnis, Michael Paulsen, Nancy Rosenblum, and Seana Shiffrin. (As we saw in Chapter 2, Justice O'Connor also flirted with this position at one time.) Their approach promises "to draw a line between [freedom of association and antidiscrimination law] that will preserve a large realm for group expression and organization while allowing the state to promote its equality objectives in the most compelling contexts."[1] A message-based approach, the neolibertarians argue, gives government the opportunity to scrutinize and reshape private speech and thereby violates the central purposes of the First Amendment. One illustration of the pathology of a message-based approach, emphasized by several of these writers and by the *Dale* Court as well, is that it produces perverse results: a group that is stridently prejudiced will receive more protection than one that is quieter about its views, and thus the rule creates an incentive to disseminate the precise prejudices that antidiscrimination laws aim to temper.

This chapter will show that the neolibertarian arguments are only slightly modified versions of old, discredited libertarian objections to the existence of any antidiscrimination law at all. The older, minimal-state libertarianism, we saw in Chapter 1, rests on three premises: (1) that a more-than-minimal state violates citizens' rights (the Rights premise), (2) that government cannot be trusted to do more than prevent force and fraud (the Distrust premise), and (3) that an unregulated private sector can be relied on to produce benign results (the Optimism premise). Libertarianism has failed as a normative theory because all three premises are often false. The neolibertarian modification is to confine all three premises so that they apply only to noncommercial associations. But even thus restricted in scope, there is no reason to think that any of them is true as a general matter.

The pressure that a message-based approach brings to bear on discriminatory associations is just what antidiscrimination law should aim at. A message-based approach does put some pressure on discriminatory associations: discrimination is not so cheap as it was before, and a group will have to decide whether discrimination is worth the added cost. But this pressure serves state interests of the highest order, and does not prevent groups with strongly held discriminatory ideas from uniting and disseminating them.

The Proposal

Whenever antidiscrimination laws have been proposed, they have been resisted on the ground that they interfere with freedom of association — that they force people to enter into transactions they do not want. Such arguments are now widely discredited with regard to race. Few people still believe that there should be a right to refuse someone a job or housing because of the color of his or her skin.

Neolibertarianism is a mutated form of a perennial type of conservative constitutionalism, one which holds that government ought not to intervene in the private sector, because to do so violates citizens' rights, because government cannot be trusted with such powers, or because the unregulated private sector is already the best of all possible worlds. The neolibertarian move is to deploy the same old arguments but to restrict their scope to apply only to noncommercial associations. The challenge for the neolibertarians is to show that the modifications rescue the arguments from the fatal flaws of their predecessors.

The newest arguments for a right against antidiscrimination law modify the older libertarian view, which had no use for the commercial/noncommercial distinction, but continue to rely on some combination of Rights, Distrust, and Optimism.

The strongest Rights-based claims after *Dale* are those developed by Michael Stokes Paulsen. He contends that the freedom of speech should be understood to include all exercises of freedom of association. The First Amendment's text "does not limit the freedom to those who speak alone,"[2] and so must include the right of groups to choose the content of their messages. "That logically entails a freedom of autonomous message formation and delivery by the group, including the right of the group to define itself — to define who will constitute the group that forms the message and the speakers who will express it on behalf of the group — and, finally, to exclude competing messages from being intermingled with the group's chosen expression."[3] These activities are not themselves speech, but they are a necessary part of the process that produces speech, and so Paulsen infers that they should also be protected from state interference.[4] Government's incompetence to regulate speech entails its incompetence to regulate the precursors of speech, such as association.

Paulsen's argument might be understood to apply only to precursors of speech that are clearly tied to the production of a specific message. But this would just give us the message-based approach of *Roberts* again, and Paulsen has bigger ambitions. If the thesis is not thus confined, it entails the unconstitutionality of the Civil Rights Act of 1964, which affected the precursors of speech by disrupting racist institutions and condemning racism as morally wrong.[5] The act played a powerful role in changing racist social norms.[6] Antidiscrimination law is not intelligible except as an effort to change such norms.[7]

Paulsen is skeptical of the diminished protection accorded to commercial speech[8] and thinks the distinction particularly problematic in the expressive association cases: "Expressive associations can have substantial commercial aspects . . . Conversely, commercial business enterprises can have substantial expressive dimensions."[9] Because Paulsen's approach is so abstract, it offers little to anchor the commercial/noncommercial distinction. He concedes that the distinction may have value because it "supplies an important, if imperfect, limiting principle that attempts to cabin government's efforts to limit the freedom of expressive association,"[10] but this implies that nothing of value would be lost if government's power to regulate associations were not "cabined" to commercial associations, but eliminated altogether.

The trouble doesn't stop with the Civil Rights Act, either. All human conduct is a precursor of speech. All government regulation affects the culture. Thus, Paulsen's theory entails the correctness of *Lochner v. New York* as well. Maximum hours laws affect attitudes toward both work and economic policy and thus have political consequences. In this respect, such laws determine the speech that will occur. This reasoning is anarchic in its implications.[11] If government cannot be trusted to regulate any of the precursors of political criticism, then government cannot be trusted to regulate anything.

A similarly broad reading of the First Amendment is implicit in the *Dale* opinion, as Richard Epstein has noted. Building on the Court's holding that an association need only engage in expression in order to be protected, he observes that businesses are constantly engaged in expressive activity, and so the logic of *Dale* applies to them as well as to noneconomic entities.[12]

The basic problem will be present in any Rights-based approach to freedom of association that tries somehow to derive the specifics of this liberty from the abstract idea of freedom itself. The resulting theory will be so abstract that there will be no traction to support the economic/noneconomic distinction, and so it will always collapse back into paleolibertarianism. The only hope for maintaining the neolibertarian position, then, is some kind of consequentialist argument. And, indeed, the most persuasive of the neolibertarians rely on some combination of Distrust and Optimism.

Dale Carpenter and Seana Shiffrin are two proponents of associational freedom whose work is driven largely by Distrust. Carpenter thoroughly catalogues the dangers of *Roberts*'s message-based approach, which requires courts to scrutinize a group's message to determine whether that message is impaired by the application of an antidiscrimination law. Such an approach, he argues, is likely to systematically punish unpopular opinions, since any doubt about a group's message will probably be resolved against such opinions. The message-based approach, he argues, underestimates the expressiveness of membership policies. It fails to notice that silence can itself be a kind of speech, as it was in the case of the BSA. And it fails to note the practical harm to an organization that can be brought about by compliance with an antidiscrimination law.[13] Shiffrin similarly worries that, under this approach, "[g]roups who tolerate or encourage within their ranks internal dissent, experimentation, or critical reexamination are more likely to lose control over their membership than those who adopt a posture of unyielding stridency."[14] It "may pressure a diverse, unfocused group that nevertheless cares to control its membership to generate artificially a set unified message that rationalizes their pattern of exclusion."[15]

A message-based approach does indeed present all these dangers. On the other hand, these specific abuses have not manifested themselves often.[16] Carpenter worries that these dangers are particularly problematic for gay organizations, but he offers no historical instance in which the message-based approach was used to such an organization's detriment.[17]

The commercial/noncommercial distinction is offered as a "compromise"[18] solution that avoids these dangers. Carpenter observes that "holding a job is more important to most people than learning morals from a scoutmaster while tying a knot in front of a campfire."[19] Shiffrin justifies the distinction on the basis of "the central importance of fair access to material resources and mechanisms of power."[20] Economic interests, which are protected by the application of antidiscrimination laws to employers and retail businesses, are indeed more important than the noneconomic interests that would be served by the application of such laws to noncommercial associations. But it does not follow that noneconomic interests are *un*important. This compromise might sensibly be adopted by a legislature. Indeed, most state legislatures *have* adopted it. But it does not follow that those who reject this compromise are violating the Constitution.

The same theme of Distrust is clear in Richard Epstein's critique of a message-based approach, though he carries it to a different conclusion than Carpenter. The BSA's policy of quietly discriminating against gays made it hard for the organization to establish its message in court, Epstein observes, but it is "the kind of studied compromise that a large and successful organization must make to stave off schism or disintegration."[21] The compromise is "more stable in practice than coherent in theory,"[22] but if greater clarity is a prerequisite for protection, then "[t]he obvious incentive is for organizations to take extreme positions in order to avoid the heavy hand of state regulation."[23] A similar concern is intimated in the *Dale* opinion: "The fact that the organization does not trumpet its views from the housetops . . . does not mean that its views receive no First Amendment protection."[24] This is a serious objection. I shall defer consideration of it until after we examine the pertinent state interests.

We already noticed that Distrust needs Optimism in order to be persuasive: even clumsy government intervention will be justified if the consequences of an unregulated market are worse. Thus, it is not surprising that the BSA's own attorney relied primarily on Optimism to make his case.

The Optimism strategy has been stressed by Professor (now Judge) Michael McConnell, who argued the case for the BSA in *Dale*. McConnell's brief claimed that private, noncommercial expressive associations have a right to choose their own members and an unqualified right to choose their leaders.[25] He has expanded on the justification for this rule in his writings outside the litigation:

If every group is internally diverse and pluralistic, reflecting the population as a whole, every group will be the same. If groups are required to accept members and appoint leaders who do not share their distinctive beliefs, their distinctive voice will be silenced. If individuals with disfavored beliefs can be forced to participate in institutions designed to mold them in accordance with the dictates of political correctness, the tapestry of pluralism will be seriously impaired. Genuine pluralism requires group difference, and maintenance of group difference requires that groups have the freedom to exclude, as well as the freedom to dissent. Freedom of association is an essential structural principle in a liberal society.[26]

What McConnell describes would indeed be a nightmare, but is it a real danger? Even New Jersey, when it applied its antidiscrimination laws to the BSA, did not say that there could be no discrimination anywhere in the state, but only that the BSA was large and unselective enough to be a public accommodation. McConnell's objection is like an argument against economic regulation that thunders about the evils of Leninism. This distrust is coupled with the optimistic assumption that in an unregulated society, associations will conform to the maximum possible extent to the beliefs of citizens.

The resemblance between McConnell's argument and old arguments for laissez-faire economics is clearest in an early article he coauthored with Judge Richard Posner. The McConnell-Posner vision is one of "a constitutionally prescribed free market for religious belief."[27] Just as an economist assumes that absent competitive distortions such as externalities, an unregulated market will allocate resources efficiently, so the theorist of religious freedom should assume that competition between religions is valuable.

The use of a free-market benchmark is important because it identifies ways in which government policy distorts (sometimes unintentionally) the pattern of economic activity, causing resources to flow from higher-valued to lower-valued uses. Similarly, the First Amendment can be understood as positing that the "market" — the realm of private choice — will reach the "best" religious results; or, more accurately, that the government has no authority to alter such results.[28]

Government should be neutral toward religion in that it should "create neither incentives nor disincentives to engage in religious activities."[29]

McConnell's argument for freedom of association closely resembles his argument for freedom of religion. In both cases, the analogy with the market is doing a lot of work. His *Dale* brief argues that "controversial questions of personal morality, often involving religious conviction, are best tested and resolved within the private marketplace of ideas, and not as the subject of government-imposed orthodoxy."[30]

In his leading article on the religion clauses, McConnell proposes to read the First Amendment to "protect against government-induced uniformity in matters of religion."[31] The baseline for the question of whether government is inhibiting or inducing religious practice, McConnell argues, should be "the hypothetical world in which individuals make decisions about religion on the basis of their own religious conscience, without the influence of government."[32] But this hypothetical world not only does not exist — it cannot be imagined. All religious choices are always already made in a political context.[33] In a world in which Christians are not permitted by the state to massacre Jews, it is inevitable that the meaning of Christianity will gradually shift, so that Christians no longer think that massacres of Jews are pleasing to God. Legislation by its nature induces uniformity. If government must play no role in the shaping of religion, then courts must invalidate the homicide statutes, which impair the formation and preservation of religions (such as that of the Aztecs) that value homicide. Any action at all by government will have some effect on religion, so absent anarchy, a world in which there is no effect whatsoever is neither attainable nor desirable.

McConnell and Posner acknowledge this.[34] The interpretation of neutrality that they advocate is one in which "effects of government action on religious practice must be minimized, and can be justified only on the basis of demonstrable and unavoidable relation to a public purpose unrelated to the religious effect."[35] Prevention of negative externalities would always satisfy this test; provision of public goods might or might not, depending on the weights of the burden on the minority and of the relative impairment of the good; paternalism and enforcement of morality should never count.[36] Unlike McConnell's approach to freedom of association, there is no talk of absolute rights.

To the extent that this argument is persuasive, it is because a quasi-libertarian argument works unusually well in the area of religion: many people believe that there is a fundamental right to follow one's religious convictions; there is ample evidence that government is incompetent to discern religious truth; and there is also much evidence that religion thrives under a nonestablishment rule.[37] The Distrust consideration is particularly powerful here. James Madison famously denounced the idea "that the Civil Magistrate is a competent Judge of Religious Truth" as "an arrogant pretension falsified by the contradictory opinions of Rulers in all ages."[38] But this incompetence does not extend to all possible matters of cultural formation.

One of the most powerful defenses of an absolute freedom of noncommercial association is Nancy Rosenblum's book *Membership and Morals.*[39] Rosenblum shows that even the most discriminatory and illiberal associations do not invariably damage liberal citizenship. For the alienated loners who join such associations, the likely alternative to illiberal participation is not liberal participation, but even more antisocial behaviors such as crime and drug addiction. Membership in illiberal groups may also strengthen some virtues of citizenship, such as hard work, economic self-sufficiency, and cooperation. Some memberships are also temporary and limited, and coexist with other identities and memberships.

Rosenblum's evidence destroys the mechanistic assumption that liberal society is undermined by all illiberal prejudices and associations within it. But to refute this claim is not to establish the opposite proposition, that such prejudices and associations never have antiliberal consequences severe enough to warrant legislative intervention. Epstein's claim that competition among groups will provide a satisfactory remedy for any pattern of exclusion, Rosenblum thinks, "applies much more convincingly to voluntary associations than it does to employment."[40] How can she know this? One would need to examine the evidence in favor of intervention in any particular case in order to determine both the benefit achieved thereby and the burden on association.

A similar combination of Optimism and Distrust appears in John McGinnis's defense of *Dale*. McGinnis thinks that *Dale* instantiates a general theme in the Rehnquist Court's jurisprudence, of promoting "decentralization and the private ordering of social norms."[41] The rule of *Dale*, he argues, prevents totalitarian domination of government over culture. The abandonment of a message-based approach "allows private associations to exert subtle social pressures through relatively quiet judgments."[42] Requiring a clear link between message and protection would create a world "where contentious political advocacy alone supplements the norms encouraged by the government."[43] And, once again, the market will fix any wrong that is done: "BSA's policy decisions are subject to a self-correcting mechanism because they put the organization at risk of losing members and civic respect."[44] This is often true of noneconomic associations. It is also often true of economic associations. Like Epstein and Paulsen, McGinnis thinks that the economic/noneconomic distinction may prove "unstable,"[45] since so much of business is expressive. It is hard to keep the logic of the argument from reaching the Civil Rights Act. Since the neolibertarian argument rests on an analogy between associations and markets, it is no surprise that the argument applies as well to markets as it does to associations.[46]

Like the arguments for laissez-faire economic policy, the Optimism argument for freedom of association overgeneralizes from what is often the case to a claim about what is always the case. Regulation of markets is indeed unnecessary and counterproductive. Except sometimes. The neolibertarians claim that the "sometimes" does not happen all that often, but this is merely a hunch. It is dangerous for such hunches to become the basis of judge-made law, particularly constitutional law that is immune to legislative reconsideration in light of experience.[47]

The next two chapters will take a closer look at the "sometimes." First, however, a bit more has to be said about the Distrust argument.

The argument just offered challenges the Optimistic story, but we have not yet addressed the Distrust problem. Absent Optimism, though, Distrust can take us to a very different judicial rule than the one contemplated by the neolibertarians.

Distrust was a pervasive theme in the Supreme Court's reasoning in *Employment Division v. Smith*.[48] In this case, the Court, largely consolidating a trend of previous cases,[49] held that the free exercise clause does not authorize the courts to carve out exemptions to generally applicable laws when such laws burden religious activities. One reason why the Court declined to protect religious activities was that a different rule would require it to assess the burden that any law placed on religious activities, which in turn would require it to scrutinize the beliefs of the religious. Justice Scalia's reservations about that procedure look a lot like Carpenter's and Epstein's reservations about a message-based approach to freedom of association:

> It is no more appropriate for judges to determine the "centrality" of religious beliefs before applying a "compelling interest" test in the free exercise field, than it would be for them to determine the "importance" of ideas before applying the "compelling interest" test in the free speech field. What principle of law or logic can be brought to bear to contradict a believer's assertion that a particular act is "central" to his personal faith? Judging the centrality of different religious practices is akin to the unacceptable "business of evaluating the relative merits of differing religious claims." . . . Repeatedly and in many different contexts, we have warned that courts must not presume to determine the place of a particular belief in a religion or the plausibility of a religious claim.[50]

The rule that remains after *Smith* protects religion only against intentional interference motivated by animus against a specific religion.[51] If one similarly distrusts judges' ability fairly to discern and weigh the importance of associations' messages, one might follow the reasoning of *Smith* by concluding that associations should have similar protection: only laws that deliberately burden them because of their viewpoint should be deemed to violate the First Amendment.[52]

Before *Dale,* of course, the Court had a more protective rule than this: if it could be shown that a antidiscrimination law burdened an association's ability to express its viewpoint, then the law would be invalid unless it was necessary to a compelling state interest. The reason for the additional protection, as noted earlier, is that some associations really are so closely connected with specific speech that the associations are practically inseparable from the speech. But deciding whether this is so in any particular case depends on a fact-specific investigation, with all the dangers of subjectivity and balancing that repulsed the Court in *Smith.*[53] The difference between the two cases is that in the case of religion, it is well settled that courts may not interpret religious doctrines.[54] But this is entailed by the requirement that government not make pronouncements of religious truth,[55] a requirement that is not relevant to most cases of freedom of association.[56]

The message-based approach does have the effect of offering protection only to the most obviously prejudiced speakers. Epstein's question deserves an answer. "Why should the First Amendment protect only the extremes of the political distribution, but not the associational preferences of large, mainstream organizations?"[57]

The answer is that social meanings are not innocuous. Antidiscrimination law presumes, and experience amply shows, that patterns of discrimination and exclusion will perpetuate themselves absent legal intervention, and that this justifies such intervention. The law is intervening to try to change social meanings. The message-based approach does put pressure on the culture to become less discriminatory, but it does so in a way respectful of speech, particularly the speech of those who most disagree with the government's position.

Jennifer Gerarda Brown argues that states should enact disclosure requirements that would require associations to disclose their discriminatory policies as the price for exemption from antidiscrimination laws. Such requirements would ensure that people know the messages that they are associating with when they join an association, and so would facilitate more meaningful associational decisions.[58] Brown's proposal is attractive (and I endorse it), but she does not notice how close we now are to the regime she proposes. The *Dale* litigation forced the BSA to be open about its discriminatory policy and thus made salient an exclusion that previously had been tacit and thus normalized.[59]

Antidiscrimination law does not defer to the market. It skews its operation in just the way that a message-based approach skews the operation of associations. Kimberly Yuracko has shown that the prohibition of sex discrimination in employment has isolated exceptions. Some of these derive from gender-based concerns of personal privacy: hospitals can discriminate in hiring nurses in maternity wards, and retirement homes can discriminate when they hire personal caregivers for their patients. More interesting is the case of businesses that sell sexual titillation. Strip clubs can discriminate when they hire strippers, but businesses are not permitted to discriminate for the sake of "plus-sex" marketing, which packages sexual titillation together with other products. To take one well-known example, airlines may not discriminate on the basis of sex in order to combine air travel with alluring flight attendants.[60] "When deciding sexual-titillation cases, courts effectively do two things: (1) they rigidly divide the work world between sex and nonsex businesses, and (2) they police the boundaries between these categories to ensure that the nonsex world does not shrink, even though it may grow."[61] This rule makes sense because the sexualization of the workplace "alters the way [women] are treated by others so that their intellectual and professional attributes are simply less likely to be recognized and encouraged."[62] Such focus on the body also has a detrimental effect on the performance of the women themselves.[63] Constricting the market makes people freer.

Like plus-sex businesses, invisible-discrimination associations aren't allowed to exist. You can avoid the application of antidiscrimination law only by openly and notoriously discriminating. But when you do that, you scare away some of the customers. This becomes a powerful incentive not to discriminate.

Does this effect itself create First Amendment difficulties? Is the state, under this rationale, suppressing speech in order to suppress its message? Carpenter correctly observes that under a message-based approach, ambiguity is likely to be construed against associations that want to discriminate.[64] More importantly, silence itself can sometimes be a message.

> Gay advocates understand that silence signals tacit disapproval of gay-rights claims, or at the very least embarrassment and shame about the subject. . . . [A]gainst the backdrop of loud, continuous, and insistent demands to discuss and take sides on gay-rights claims, a steadfast refusal to talk at all about the issue is hardly neutral. It is itself a position, a "message." It is like the schoolchild who remains silent while students all around him recite the Pledge of Allegiance. . . . Preserving traditional sexual morality is the goal; silence is the method. We may not like the goal or the method. But if the First Amendment secures some space in which to develop one's own identity, it surely guarantees enough to prevent the evolution of that identity in a direction the state demands.[65]

But the freedom of speech doesn't mean a right to engage in otherwise prohibited conduct in order to send a message, nor does it authorize one to disregard generally applicable laws whenever compliance with them will be taken by onlookers to send a message.

A law that precludes silent discrimination does not necessarily burden speech. Silence is not always a message. At least some entities that discriminate are not thinking about sending any message at all. An absolute right of noncommercial entities to associate, William Marshall observes, "is overbroad because it protects discrimination wholly removed from the expressive goals of the organization."[66] So when the message-based approach collides with the determined silence of the BSA, the collision is less like *West Virginia v. Barnette*[67] (which found a constitutional right not to be compelled to speak) than it is like *Clark v. Community for Creative Non-Violence*[68] (which found that there was no right to violate a law against camping in a park in order to send a message): the First Amendment does not bar application of a law that prohibits conduct that is not itself inherently communicative, even if the defendant engages in the conduct for communicative reasons, as long as the law does not define the prohibited conduct by reference to the viewpoint that is communicated.

Does it matter that government's purpose is to shape the culture? But the law does this all the time. When people are forbidden to discriminate, this makes it more likely that they will develop less discriminatory attitudes. When people are forbidden to steal, this makes it more likely that they will develop greater respect for others' property. When any conduct is prohibited, preferences tend to adapt so that the conduct is no longer desired. These effects are not unintended. The fact that they are intended does not mean that the laws violate the First Amendment. People's preferences are inevitably shaped in nonrational ways by their environment, and law is part of that environment. Typically, neither racists nor nonracists arrive at their positions through a process of rational deliberation. Antidiscrimination law redirects these nonrational processes in a way that ameliorates severe and pervasive harms. As George Sher asks, "exactly what is disrespectful about taking (benign) advantage of a causal process that would occur anyway?"[69]

A message-based rule, in short, raises the cost of discrimination. Raising the cost of discrimination means that you will get less of it. This effect can already be seen in the aftermath of *Dale*, when the BSA suffered a decline in its membership. In the course of litigation — and certainly once the case was over — the BSA became so associated with discrimination against gays that the organization now almost certainly could satisfy the *Roberts* test. Its fate is a warning to other groups. Discrimination isn't free. Nor should it be.

5

Is the BSA Being as Bad as Racists?

Judging the BSA's Antigay Policy

All that we have considered so far is whether there should be an absolute right to discriminate. But what about the other side of the equation — the state interest in regulating private associations? Why should the state want to do this? What legitimate reason could there be for the state to interfere with the internal membership decisions of a private association such as the BSA?

The BSA's discriminatory policy raises a moral concern. This chapter lays that concern out in detail. The next chapter will work out its institutional implications.

The moral status of the BSA's policy has become an object of intense debate. The organization's victory in *Dale* has been costly. The policy of discriminating against gays was not widely known until the litigation publicized it. In the fairly short time since then, membership has fallen by almost 15 percent (from 2000 to 2007).[1] Some corporate donors, such as CVS, American Airlines, Wells Fargo, J. P.

Morgan, IBM, and Levi Strauss, as well as many United Way chapters, have cut off their funding of the BSA.[2] So many public schools have denied the organization the right to meet on their property that it had to seek an act of Congress for relief.[3] Opposition to the BSA's antigay policy has also arisen within the BSA itself (see Chapter 6), and this opposition has grown to become a social movement.[4]

The stakes are high. The BSA is a major American institution. The organization is old, rich, and huge. It was founded in 1910 and chartered by Congress in 1916. It has an endowment of $609 million. In 2006, it had $194 million in revenues and an operating surplus of $5.7 million.[5] It has had more than 110 million youth members, including 2.9 million today. At the time of the *Dale* litigation, 50 percent of all American boys between the ages of seven and ten were Cub Scouts, and 20 percent between eleven and eighteen were Boy Scouts.[6]

Is there a moral principle that condemns the BSA's policy? The most damaging charge against the exclusion is that it is morally equivalent to racial discrimination.[7] But this analogy is ambiguous because it may rest on either of two moral claims.

One familiar way of understanding the charge is that racism wrongfully hurts people who do not deserve it, and that the exclusion of gays does this, too. In the same way that black people found themselves the object of false ideas of racial inferiority, gay people find themselves the object of false ideas of homosexual inferiority.

This claim has persuaded many. I have propounded it myself.[8] It depends, however, on the acceptance of a controversial prior claim — that homosexual sex is in no way inferior to heterosexual sex. This dependence weakens the power of the racism analogy. Many Americans think that homosexual sex is morally unacceptable,[9] and for them the analogy can have no power. The BSA has stated that it is "committed to the concept that sexual intimacy is the sole providence [*sic*] of a man and a woman within the bonds of marriage."[10] This moral view is held by a number of the major American religious denominations, and in a pluralistic society, there should be room for people to hold such views. If the criticism of the BSA rests entirely upon disagreement with its moral beliefs about sexuality, then the organization's response is a fair one: "We respect other people's rights to hold differing opinions and ask that they respect ours."[11]

There is, however, another way of understanding the racism analogy, one that is not contingent on judgments about its effect. This second and stronger account of the analogy is, if it is sustainable, far more damaging to the BSA. It begins by observing that racism contradicts the foundations of human rights because racism holds that some people are intrinsically inferior in worth. Suppose that it could be shown that the BSA's policy similarly treated gay people as intrinsically inferior. This showing would provide a reason to condemn the policy that would not be contingent on any view of the morality of homosexual conduct. It would imply that there is something categorically immoral about the policy, in the same way that racism is categorically immoral. It would mean that even those who agree with the BSA's views on sexual morality should condemn its policy of excluding gays.

In this chapter, I will argue that the second racism analogy is a valid one. My argument has three steps. First, I will identify what is essentially morally malign about racism: the stigmatizing of people as intrinsically inferior. Next, I will demonstrate that some, but not all, objections to homosexuality do the same thing and are similarly malign. Finally, I will show that the BSA's policy falls within this malign category of antigay positions.

This book deliberately takes no position on the morality of homosexual conduct because it is addressed to an audience that is deeply divided on that question. Even those who condemn homosexual conduct almost always concede the unfairness of stigmatizing people for their homosexual status. Thus, even if it were stipulated that homosexual conduct is per se immoral, the BSA's policy would be wrong for the same reasons that racism is wrong.

Some readers will be troubled by this stipulation, even for the sake of argument.[12] Perhaps it is possible to hate the sin and love the sinner, but if I am the object of this kind of love, I am likely to notice primarily that you hate everything *about* me, including the things that I most care about, and that the object of your Procrustean hospitality is some invisible essence with no discernible connection to my particular self.[13] But this objection presupposes that my choices are morally permissible ones. Some unchosen desires should never be fulfilled. The idea of human rights does not entail the view that homosexual acts are morally permissible. In a world in which the idea of human rights has a much larger constituency than the idea that homosexual conduct is legitimate, it is important to show that some gay rights claims do not depend on the latter idea. The case against the BSA's policy, for example, does not depend on that idea.

The traditional moralists' distinction between homosexual status and homosexual conduct is rife with difficulties. It promises gay people a respected status in the community, but at a heavy price: they must hide their desires, never act upon them, and abstain from sex for the rest of their lives. This is a poor bargain, and increasing numbers of gay people refuse it. Nonetheless, traditionalists' insistence on the distinction imposes obligations upon them. The distinction is what separates them from the lowest order of bigots, the racists and Nazis.

For this reason, they should be held to their promised bargain. Much is revealed when they stop paying attention to it.

This chapter attempts to extend the reach of practical philosophy to a neglected set of issues. Practical philosophy tends to focus either on individual ethics or on politics. Critical evaluation of social movements that seek anything other than state action is rare. The state is not, however, the only means by which people act collectively, and ethical standards apply to other forms of collective action as well.

Racism and Agency

What is wrong with racism and racially discriminatory practices? I begin with a syllogism:

Major premise: It is unjust to stigmatize a person for reasons that have nothing to do with that person's choices. Moral blameworthiness intelligibly attaches only to a person who has behaved differently from the way he or she should have and could have. George Sher has argued persuasively that the idea of desert is inextricably linked to the idea of free agency: if we deserve anything, this is because our free choices typically encompass the expected consequences of those choices as well as our immediate doings, so that the value of any choice carries over to its expected consequences.[14] It follows that one cannot deserve something that is completely unrelated to one's agency.

Two clarifications may be helpful. First, the point is not that one should never *differentiate* on the basis of immutable characteristics. We do this all the time when, for example, we deny pilot licenses to blind people. But such denial does not *stigmatize* or *blame* the blind people. It does not treat them as pariahs or as objects of disgust.[15]

Second, the moral objection to the unjust ascription of blame is not a categorical one. Sometimes such unjust ascription is a necessary effect of an otherwise justified policy, as when a mildly retarded student who could not have done better is held back in grade school. In such cases, some overriding social benefit must be present to excuse the injustice that has been done. The injustice remains an injustice.

Minor premise: Racially discriminatory beliefs and practices stigmatize black people as objects of stigma and blame without reference to any willed acts of theirs. This can happen in several ways. Anthony Appiah distinguishes between two different kinds of racist ideas. One, which he calls "extrinsic racism," claims that race entails morally relevant qualities, such as honesty or courage (or the lack thereof), which are uncontroversially proper bases for treating people differently. "Intrinsic racism," on the other hand, holds "that each race has a different moral status, quite independent of the moral characteristics entailed by its racial essence."[16] Intrinsic racism, unlike extrinsic racism, is not rebuttable by evidence. It holds some people inferior regardless of what they think or do. It thereby directly contradicts the major premise of the syllogism stated above. The issue is a bit more complex with extrinsic racism, which relies on claims that would be relevant if true. What is remarkable about extrinsic racism, Appiah observes, is that it is typically the product of a cognitive incapacity: "extrinsic racists, however intelligent or otherwise well informed, often fail to treat evidence against the theoretical propositions of extrinsic racism dispassionately."[17] Their conflict with the major premise is this: they wrongly stigmatize people who in fact do not have the negative moral traits that are attributed to them. The two typically are psychologically linked (though Appiah does not explore this link in any detail).

Absent intrinsic racism, it is doubtful that people would so easily accept the stereotypes that are the basis of extrinsic racism.

Conclusion: These beliefs and practices are morally wrong. They assign stigma where stigma does not belong.

There are powerful tendencies in many, perhaps all, cultures to attach stigma inappropriately, to conditions that do not arise from one's will. Anthropologist Mary Douglas's classic study of pollution offers one explanation for this phenomenon. Douglas observes that the idea of pollution exists in all cultures. Everywhere, she argues, "dirt is essentially disorder. There is no such thing as absolute dirt: it exists in the eye of the beholder."[18] Eliminating it "is not a negative movement, but a positive effort to organise the environment."[19] "Dirt is the by-product of a systematic ordering and classification of matter, in so far as ordering involves rejecting inappropriate elements."[20] Pollution rules thus are comprehensible only in light of their cultural context. "For the only way in which pollution ideas make sense is in reference to a total structure of thought whose key-stone, boundaries, margins and internal lines are held in relation by rituals of separation."[21]

The inappropriate things sought to be eliminated are sometimes human beings. "Thus in some West African tribes the rule that twins should be killed at birth eliminates a social anomaly, if it is held that two humans could not be born from the same womb at the same time."[22] Whether individuals are understood as polluting would seem to depend on whether the total structure of thought deems them anomalous.

A problem that pollution ideas entail for contemporary society is that such ideas may contradict the modern idea that blameworthiness can arise only from one's will. Douglas notes that the early Christian church had to struggle against the idea that a blameless person, such as a leper or a cripple, could become ritually unclean.[23] Yet the culture continues to entertain organizing ideas in light of which some people are seen as unclean and polluting. Racism is the obvious example. Chief Justice Roger Taney of the U.S. Supreme Court wrote in the 1857 *Dred Scott* case that the pre-Civil War U.S. Constitution enshrined the view that blacks were "beings of an inferior order, and altogether unfit to associate with the white race, either in social or political relations; and so far inferior, that they had no rights which the white man was bound to respect."[24] Charles Black observes that the entire structure of racial segregation in the post-Civil War South was predicated on the idea of blacks as contaminating: "It is actionable defamation in the South to call a white man a Negro. A small proportion of Negro 'blood' puts one in the inferior race for segregation purposes; this is the way in which one deals with a taint, such as a carcinogene in cranberries."[25] Richard Wasserstrom noted that the system of segregation treated blacks as "the sorts of creatures who could and would contaminate white persons if they came into certain kinds of contact with them — in the bathroom, at the dinner table, or in bed, although it was appropriate for blacks to prepare or handle food, and even to nurse white infants."[26] Douglas's explanation of pollution ideas makes sense of these puzzling distinctions. The point was the maintenance of certain valued social categories, which were threatened when blacks left their appropriate place. And the trouble with all this was that the system of segregation was massively unjust. At the heart of the system of segregation is a set of beliefs that label some people as intrinsically inferior, as contaminated, for reasons that have nothing to do with their own choices.

The conclusion that a racist system is unjust has ethical implications. Prejudices cannot persist in a society unless practices maintain them. They depend on habitualized actions that pass on the prejudices to the next generation. Loci of official power may play an important role in reproducing these prejudices, but this need not be the case; the work may be done entirely by private actors.[27] If you accept the syllogism with which I began, and if your culture assigns blame in ways that are unrelated to the will, then you will disagree with those aspects of the culture and want to change them. And that will require you to do what you can to change the practices that maintain the prejudice.

This conclusion is, I believe, widely though unreflectively understood. An antiracist ethic has emerged in American society. Almost no one any longer is overtly racist.[28] Yet most Americans understand that racism persists and regard it as a problem.[29] There is an emerging social norm of signals, whereby one is expected to avoid speech and conduct that signifies racism.[30] This norm has become one of the most potent cultural weapons against racism.

In the absence of overt racism, judgments must be made as to whether any particular actor is promulgating racism despite that actor's avowals to the contrary. The judgments involve both intentions and effects, but their primary focus is on social meaning: does an actor's conduct have a conventional meaning that signifies prejudice against blacks?[31]

For an example of the kind of reasoning that is required, consider the case of Bob Jones University. As the Supreme Court noted, "the sponsors of the University genuinely believe[d] that the Bible forbids interracial dating and marriage. To effectuate these views, Negroes were completely excluded until 1971. From 1971 to May 1975, the University accepted no applications from unmarried Negroes, but did accept applications from Negroes married within their race."[32] After the law forbade discrimination in admissions, the school continued to prohibit interracial dating and marriage. The Internal Revenue Service then decided that the university was not entitled to federal tax exemption because of this racially discriminatory policy, and the Supreme Court upheld that decision.

The idea that interracial dating and marriage are immoral is not itself necessarily malign. It does not *logically* imply the inferiority of blacks, but it has a powerful cultural association with this implication. Historically, the miscegenation taboo is close to the psychological core of American racism. It notoriously connotes a narrative in which black men represent a dangerous, predatory, uncontrollable sexuality, and white women represent a fragile, asexual purity, the protection of which is the special duty of white men.[33] Chief Justice Taney recognized the miscegenation prohibition as a "stigma, of the deepest degradation . . . fixed upon the whole [black] race."[34] The power of that cultural association was enough to justify condemnation of the university for perpetuating racism.

Thus, when the university reentered the public eye after presidential candidate George W. Bush held a rally there, the national reaction against the policy became overwhelming. Even the most conservative politicians denounced the policy.[35] Bob Jones University insisted that its views had nothing to do with racism, but no one was convinced. In March 2000, the pressure of public opinion induced the school to abandon the prohibition.[36]

This public pressure was not unfair. The university's policy breached the social norm just described. Disregard of that norm may reasonably be perceived as endorsing a racist message and revealing one's own racism. Racism is now itself treated as a kind of pollution, and social norms operate to expel it. Unlike racist pollution ideas, this antiracism norm does not blame anyone for anything beyond his or her control, but it does have costs. It uses social pressure to enforce a kind of social conformity. These costs are justified, however. The transformation of racial attitudes, to the point where overt racism has been almost universally repudiated, is a great social good.

The Variety of Antigay Attitudes

It is sometimes alleged that antigay attitudes are morally equivalent to racism. As I noted at the beginning, this may simply mean that these attitudes unjustifiably harm gay people. This charge is a serious one. It is not a light thing to damage people's lives, even if one does so on the basis of negligence or erroneous moral views. But the racism analogy may mean something deeper: that these attitudes contradict foundational ideas of human rights. This latter category of equivalence, I will now argue, does hold with respect to some antigay attitudes.

The terms "gay" or "homosexual" are ambiguous. When used to describe people, each word can have at least two different meanings. These words may refer to a person who habitually engages in sexual activity with people of the same sex. A person who performs same-sex sex acts is "gay" in the same way that a person who performs acts of carpentry is a carpenter. Or the term may refer to a person's desires. Gay people, according to this second meaning, are those who "have a predominant erotic attraction to others of the same sex. Their sexual fantasies are either entirely or almost entirely directed toward other [people of the same sex], and have been so since childhood. Because sexual behavior may be inhibited by societal pressure or by internal conflict, a [person] need not engage in sexual activity to be homosexual."[37]

When speakers state that they condemn homosexuals, therefore, they may be saying either of two things. They may be saying that they think that sex acts with people of the same sex are wrong. Or they may be saying that they regard people who experience homosexual desire as inferior, degraded people. Some people do regard gay people as beings of an inferior order, unfit to associate with others, who have no rights that others are bound to respect.

The latter attitude is not hard to find in contemporary American culture. It is perhaps best exemplified by those who violently attack strangers whom they believe to be gay. Attacks on gays bespeak an astonishing rage, often involving torture and mutilation. Such attacks are common and constantly occur throughout the United States.[38] Gordon Allport's classic study of prejudice notes that when hate-motivated violence takes place, its perpetrators tend to be acting on attitudes that are held in milder form throughout the culture in which they have been socialized.[39]

Although few Americans actually engage in violence against gays, many more dislike them intensely. Gays are among the least liked groups in the United States, according to Kenneth Sherrill's analysis of the "feeling thermometers" of the American National Election Study. Respondents were asked to rate their feelings toward a variety of groups on a scale of 0 to 100. In four surveys spanning a ten-year period, the lowest score, zero, was consistently assigned by more respondents to gays and lesbians than to any other group; next in order were illegal immigrants, people on welfare, and Christian fundamentalists. (In 1994, the most recent year, 28.2 percent assigned gays a zero ranking; as compared with 24.2 percent for the next most unpopular group, illegal immigrants; and 9.1 percent for the third most unpopular group, people on welfare. The figure for blacks was 2.0 percent.) Sherrill concludes that "such hostility does not face any other group in the electorate."[40] The hostility is not only intense, but widespread. Gays and lesbians also have consistently received one of the lowest mean feeling thermometer scores, though in recent years they have escaped the lowest average rating by being two to four points above illegal immigrants. "Among American citizens included in these studies only lesbians and gay men were the objects of cold feelings from a majority of Americans."[41]

More recent data show some improvement. Morris Fiorina's review in 2006 found that the proportion of Americans giving gay people a zero rating "has steadily declined, from almost a third in 1988 to less than 10 percent in 2000, before rising slightly in 2004 amid the controversy over gay marriage. Along with this sharp decline in extreme dislike, the average ratings of gays and lesbians have climbed significantly in the past fifteen years."[42] But these recent data should not be overread. Negative feelings that are as deeply rooted as this one do not just disappear, even if they are consciously repudiated. Compare the case of race. Almost no one is willing to admit to racism today; yet it continues to unconsciously affect decision-making in countless ways, from employment decisions to political advertisements.[43]

The idea that gays are inferior human beings is not the only reason they are discriminated against, but it is plainly one of the reasons. Perhaps the most direct window into American culture is its ordinary language. Richard Mohr notes that the English language does not treat gay people merely as persons who engage in certain sexual activities.

With the apparent exception of "cocksucker," no widespread anti-gay slur gives any indication that its censure is directed at sex acts rather than despised social status. Group-directed slurs (dyke, queer, fag) place gays in a significant social category along with blacks (nigger, shine, shitskin), other racial groups (chink), women (cunt, gash), various ethnic groups (wop, dago, gook, jap, JAP, mick, kike) . . . They do not place gays in the same category as liars, hypocrites, murderers, and thieves —

those who commit immoral and criminal actions and yet for whom culture in no case has coined group-based invectives. This schema of slurs strongly suggests that gays are held to be immoral because they are hated, rather than hated because they are immoral.[44]

Even homosexuals who do not act on, or even who openly repudiate, their inclinations still bear the stigma of their status, if it is known. In 1976, presidential candidate Jimmy Carter told an interviewer: "I've looked on a lot of women with lust. I've committed adultery in my heart many times. This is something God recognizes I will do — and I have done it — and God forgives me for it."[45] The statement caused a minor flap at the time, but Carter went on to win the election. Imagine the reaction if he had said that he had looked on a lot of men with lust.

The idea of gay people as contaminants who need to be rooted out of society was once conventional wisdom. Ostracism for being gay is a central signifier of the stigmatized status of gays — at least as central as the interracial marriage taboo is for the stigmatized status of blacks. In 1953, President Dwight D. Eisenhower issued an executive order barring homosexuals from all federal jobs, and the FBI initiated a broad system of surveillance to keep homosexuals off the federal payroll. Corporations under government contract applied the administration's security provisions to their own employees, and many states and municipalities followed the federal government's lead, while also enforcing similar standards in the licensing of many professions. One study in the mid-1950s estimated that over 12.6 million workers, more than 20 percent of the labor force, faced loyalty-security investigations as a condition of employment.[46]

The closest thing to a canonical rationale for this pervasive discrimination was set forth in 1950 by a Senate committee that investigated

the employment of "homosexuals and other moral perverts" in government. Homosexuals, the committee concluded, lacked "emotional
stability" because "indulgence in acts of sex perversion weakens the
moral fiber of an individual to a degree that he is not suitable for a
position of responsibility." Even one "sex pervert in a Government
agency," the committee warned,

> tends to have a corrosive influence upon his fellow employees.
> These perverts will frequently attempt to entice normal indi-
> viduals to engage in perverted practices. This is particularly
> true in the case of young and impressionable people who might
> come under the influence of a pervert. . . . One homosexual can
> pollute a Government office.[47]

The bizarre fantasies in the Senate report are analogous to what Appiah calls extrinsic racism — empirical investigation is necessary in
order to reveal that they are false — but as in the race case, something
analogous to intrinsic racism, a hostility to gays as such, is probably a
necessary cause of such fantasies being so readily accepted by otherwise reasonable people.

The language of pollution is revealing. In light of the narrative of
inevitable and universal heterosexuality that is integral to many people's gender identity, gay people appear as anomalous as those West
African twins who, Douglas observed, were so disturbing that they
had to be killed at birth.

The stigma against gay people is today most profound among
adolescents. A study of harassment in American high schools found
that the most upsetting type of harassment was to be called gay.[48] One
national survey of males aged fifteen to nineteen found that 89 percent
thought that the idea of homosexual sexual activity was "disgusting,"

and only 12 percent were sure that they could befriend an openly gay male.[49] Students are often conspicuously cruel to peers whom they perceive as gay. Students thought to be gay are often publicly humiliated, threatened with harm, spit at, pushed, and physically attacked. Adults in authority often do nothing about the harassment, and sometimes they blame the victims.[50]

Gay adolescents often are rejected, not only by their peers, but by their parents as well.[51] This extreme rejection and isolation produces a disproportionately high incidence of suicide attempts.[52] One study found that such attempts were associated with "reliance on social support from people who rejected them because of their sexual orientation."[53]

Gay youth have the option of keeping their sexuality secret from everyone, but this secrecy has psychic costs of its own. The fear of discovery becomes an integral part of their lives, and the constant feeling of isolation often leads to clinical depression.[54] Suicide attempts "occurred most often before [gay youth] acknowledged or disclosed their sexual identities to others."[55]

The prejudice against gays regards them as in some ways even more polluting than racism regarded blacks. Gays are traditionally entitled to no legitimized place at all in society.[56] Martha Nussbaum observes that the judge's famous speech at Oscar Wilde's sentencing for sodomy, one of the most prominent legal texts in the history of homosexuality, "treats the prisoners as objects of disgust, vile contaminants who are not really people, and who therefore need not be addressed as if they were people."[57] From this it is not very far to Heinrich Himmler's speech to his SS generals, in which he explained that the medieval German practice of drowning gay men in bogs "was no punishment, merely the extermination of an abnormal life. It had to be removed just as we [now] pull up stinging nettles, toss them on a heap, and burn them."[58]

All this is, however, only part of the story. Many people hold the traditional view that homosexual acts are per se worthless and harmful, and that "a life involving homosexual conduct is bad even for anyone unfortunate enough to have innate or quasi-innate homosexual inclinations."[59] As I noted at the outset, many (myself among them) think that this view is mistaken and destructive. It does not, however, contradict the syllogism stated at the beginning of this chapter. The value of homosexual conduct is not deducible from the idea that desert arises from the will, and the condemnation of that conduct does not contradict the idea that desert arises from the will in the way that intrinsic racism does.

It is therefore unfair to suggest that the traditionalist view is morally equivalent to racism. Many traditionalists have even recognized the existence of prejudices against gay status and have repudiated it. The Catholic Church, for example, has condemned antigay prejudice while maintaining its condemnation of homosexual activity.[60] The church's doctrine does not entail that a person is morally defective and unclean merely because of homosexual desire. Quite the contrary: "the particular inclination of the homosexual person is not a sin."[61] Many other defenders of the traditional prohibition of homosexual conduct have gone to considerable lengths to disavow and condemn prejudice against gays.[62]

Implicit in these pronouncements is a norm analogous to the antiracist norm considered earlier. One ought to avoid speech and conduct that signifies prejudice against gay people. The case for such a norm is as strong in this context as in that of race. In both cases, the prejudice is categorically wrong but is pervasive in the culture, and a norm that opposes it is the most promising way to eliminate it. These writers understand that their views can easily be mistaken for the prejudice against gays, and that this state of affairs creates some affirmative duty to dissociate themselves from that prejudice.[63]

This conclusion should provide some badly needed common ground in the culture wars.[64] Americans are divided about the acceptability of homosexual conduct, but they are united around the idea that desert is based on one's will. The condemnation of racism is no longer controversial. Similarly, the rejection of hateful antigay ideology is a cause that even the traditionalists should unhesitatingly join.

Gay People and the BSA

We now return to the question with which we began. Is there any evidence to support the charge that the BSA's exclusion of gays is morally equivalent to racism? Does the BSA stigmatize the status of being gay?

The dispute that led to the Supreme Court decision began when the BSA revoked James Dale's membership after a newspaper story (which did not mention his affiliation with the BSA) identified him as an officer of his college's lesbian and gay student organization. When Dale, who had been a member of the BSA since he was eight years old, wrote to inquire why he was expelled, he was told that the BSA "specifically forbid[s] membership to homosexuals."[65]

The BSA claimed that Dale's continued membership would contradict the organization's moral teachings because he disagreed with those teachings. But the BSA's decision to terminate Dale was not, and could not have been, based on his beliefs. When they threw him out, they did not know anything about his beliefs. All they knew was that he had identified himself as gay.

The BSA also said that it believed that "homosexual conduct is inconsistent with the requirement in the Scout Oath that a Scout be morally straight and in the Scout Law that a Scout be clean in word and deed."[66] But the BSA didn't know anything about Dale's conduct, either. They terminated him without making any effort to find out about either his beliefs or his behavior. They threw him out for *being* gay.[67]

The basis of the BSA's exclusionary policy was later made starkly clear by the case of Leonard Lanzi, who was for many years executive director of the Los Padres Council of the BSA in California. At a meeting of the Santa Barbara Board of Supervisors, where the board was considering whether to revoke the BSA's lease at a municipal meeting house, he defended the BSA: "I am a private person, and I am gay. I uphold the Boy Scouts' policies. I would not work for the Boy Scouts if I did not know that they save lives." The BSA promptly fired him.[68] The fact that he came out as gay while defending the organization was not enough, evidently, to purge the stain of homosexuality. Once more, Lanzi's beliefs and conduct were irrelevant.[69]

The BSA's declarations of policy make clear that the exclusion is not based on belief or conduct but simply on the status of being gay. As one of the earliest position statements put it:

> The Boy Scouts of America has always reflected the expectations that Scouting families have had for the organization. We do not believe that homosexuals provide a role model consistent with these expectations. Accordingly, we do not allow for the registration of avowed homosexuals as members or as leaders of the BSA.[70]

The present position is that "an avowed homosexual cannot serve as a role model for the values of the Oath and Law."[71]

Discrimination against gay people as such, without reference to their conduct or beliefs, is, as a matter of cultural fact, closely associated with the idea of involuntary pollution. The association is at least as strong as that between the miscegenation taboo that Bob Jones University enforced and the prejudice against blacks.

The BSA would doubtless respond that I have misinterpreted its message. The organization has never overtly endorsed the view that gay people are intrinsically inferior. But this fact alone cannot dispel the concern that it is promoting the view that gay people are polluted. Bob Jones University did not overtly endorse racism, either. The question is not whether the leadership is pure in heart, but whether it is using its enormous cultural power in a way that reinforces a pollution-based prejudice. The answer depends on whether the interpretation of the policy that I have suggested is the most accurate description of its cultural meaning.[72]

The BSA's reticence about explaining its identity-based discrimination appears to be the result of two considerations. The first is that the organization does not want to teach anything about sexuality. Its stated position is that "boys should learn about sex and family life from their parents, consistent with their spiritual beliefs."[73] The second is that, as the statements already quoted indicate, the BSA does not consider gay men to be suitable role models for boys.

The second policy raises the question of why men who simply identify as gay, without indicating anything about their beliefs or conduct, are excluded. The BSA might respond that identity, belief, and conduct here merge, so that one can exclude people on the basis of their gay identity without regarding them as intrinsically inferior. The BSA might think that gay people who agree with the organization's moral views will remain closeted.[74] When charged with identity-based discrimination, the BSA's counsel shrewdly replied that "in other contexts, gay rights advocates (including respondent's counsel of record and many of the amici and their counsel) have consistently argued that 'coming out' is an expressive and political act,"[75] and quoted Nan Hunter's claim that "'identity' is a multilayered concept" and that "[s]elf-representation of one's sexual identity necessarily includes a message that one has not merely come out, but that one intends to be out — to act on and live out that identity."[76]

The BSA might also imagine that identity overlaps completely with belief because gay people can become heterosexual by a sheer act of will. This notion has increasingly captured the imagination of the Protestant religious right in America, which now sponsors a substantial "ex-gay" submovement.[77] The idea that sexual preference is easily changed is a delusion,[78] but it does not contradict the idea that desert arises from the will.

Finally, the BSA might say that it is simply responding to the demands of its members, who will not tolerate gay people in the organization. This is a weaker justification than the others. It doesn't explain all the pertinent facts, notably the willingness of the national organization to do battle with local branches over the issue.[79] A local-option rule would be a better way to make sure that parents' preferences were honored.[80] Even if it is accepted, this justification for the BSA's policy proves too much. The BSA once used a similar rationale for the segregation and even exclusion of black troops.[81]

Perhaps the BSA could tell a story that would dissociate the organization from antigay prejudice. But it has not made even a token effort to do so. The BSA does not appear to care much whether it is implying that gays are intrinsically inferior. This insouciance conveys its own message.

The BSA is now the single largest entity in the United States that excludes gay people on the basis of their identity, and it justifies this exclusion on the basis of gays' own purported moral failings.[82] It is a statistical certainty that tens of thousands of the boys who are Boy Scouts will grow up to be gay.[83] We have already reviewed the devastating consequences that result when gay youth are forced to lie and hide their identities, which is precisely what the BSA's policy requires of the gay adolescents who discover their sexuality when they are already members. Defenders of the BSA emphasize (what this book does not deny) the good that Scouting does, the valuable experiences and skills that members acquire. But these very virtues can make the program poisonous for some. The pressure on gay teenagers to hide, and the sense that their secret makes them intrinsically worthless, is more intense the more they already value and trust the adults who, they discover, reject and ostracize gay people.

It is possible to address the needs and vulnerabilities of these youth without holding that homosexual conduct is morally licit. The National Conference of Catholic Bishops, for example, has urged parents not to break off contact with gay children and has declared that "God does not love someone any less simply because he or she is homosexual."[84]

The contrast between the Catholics and the BSA is striking. At the beginning of this chapter, I conceded that the unjust ascription of stigma might be justifiable by some overriding benefit. The overriding benefit that defenders of the BSA are most likely to invoke is the reinforcement of the moral position (which they take to be correct) that homosexual conduct is morally unacceptable. But the Catholics show that one can maintain this position while scrupulously following the norm against reinforcing antigay prejudice. The BSA, on the other hand, cannot be bothered. After the Rhode Island Medical Society unanimously approved a resolution saying that the BSA's ban on gays would increase the risk of teen suicide, a spokesman for the

BSA would say only that gay youths had other options: "There are other organizations that these kids can be a member of."[85] The trouble, of course, is that (as James Dale's example shows) a boy does not know whether he is gay when he decides to join Cub Scouting.

The BSA is a far more potent and malign cultural force than Bob Jones University. BJU has made some effort to disavow racism.[86] A black student who enrolls there knows what he or she is getting into. And BJU is a marginal institution in American life, with only about five thousand students.[87] The social norm against promoting prejudices is largely justified by its consequences: the norm will help to prevent the destructive dissemination of those prejudices. The norm is therefore stronger when brought to bear on large, powerful entities that play a major role in shaping American culture. If it was worthwhile for public pressure to induce BJU to change its policy, then a fortiori, similar pressure should be brought to bear on the BSA.[88]

Has the BSA violated an antihomophobia norm that is as valid as the widely recognized antiracist norm? I have argued that there is an affirmative obligation, widely understood, to avoid endorsing racist ideas, and that conspicuous disregard of this obligation sends a racist message and is generally taken to reveal one's own racism. There should be, I have argued, a similar obligation to dissociate oneself from antigay prejudice. This obligation is particularly strong for those who work with children, who are the principal victims (and the principle enforcers!) of this prejudice. The BSA leadership does not seem to be concerned at all that the organization's policies communicate to society in general and to its young members in particular the idea that gay people are defective, unclean, and contaminating. The BSA's indifference to the well-being of its own members, youth in whose upbringing they participate, suggests that its heart may not be so pure after all.

The BSA is being, in important respects, the moral equivalent of racists. This state of affairs should stop. Different people are doing different things to try to bring it to an end. As I noted at the outset, some are cutting ties with the organization, while others are trying to work within the organization to change it.

Albert Hirschman's classic study of responses to organizational failure notes that there are two complementary responses to such failure: one can exit from the organization, as consumers characteristically do when a product in a market declines in quality, or one can remain within the organization and dissent, as characteristically happens within political units.[89] Hirschman concludes that there is no single optimal mix of exit and voice, because both strategies can be co-opted by management, which will "strain to strip the members-customers of the weapons which they can wield, be they exit or voice, and to convert, as it were, what should be a feedback into a safety valve."[90] Voice can become ineffective blowing off of steam that placates dissenters. Exit can rid management of troublemakers. Both phenomena are observable in the BSA case.

It is commonly said that those who disagree with the BSA's policies need not be members. Exit is a common method of dissent and the characteristic means of control in free markets. But as Hirschman observes, when an organization provides a public good, it is not really possible to exit.[91] One can resign from the BSA, but one must still live in a regime in which the only boys' organization with quasi-official status publicly stands for the proposition that gay people are inherently defective and contaminating.

The BSA is feeling pressure both from within and from without. This pressure ought to continue. Now that the Supreme Court has disabled the state from intervening, the only hope for significant change is a self-conscious social movement.

6

Why Regulate the BSA?

The previous chapter considered the evidence that the BSA is engaged in morally malign discrimination — discrimination that is as wrongful as racist discrimination. This argument leaves unresolved the question of whether it is appropriate for the law to intervene against the organization. Quite a lot of morally problematic conduct is not suitable for legal regulation. Why should the law be involved here?

The question of the law's legitimate interests bears directly on the question of how broad the freedom of association ought to be. As William Marshall observes, "[t]he definitional questions of where a liberty interest begins and a state interest ends are often interrelated."[1] The Supreme Court's opinion in *Dale* declares that "[t]he state interests embodied in New Jersey's public accommodations law do not justify such a severe intrusion on the Boy Scouts' rights to freedom of association,"[2] but, remarkably, it never says what these interests are. The BSA question presents a useful case study of the relevant interests and therefore of the costs of a broad judicial protection of the right of associations to exclude. Perhaps the costs are worth it. But one cannot tell unless one knows what those costs are.

The BSA's case seemed to the Court to provide the strongest justification for an expanded freedom of association. Indeed, given the uncertainty of the reach of the opinion, perhaps all one can say with confidence about *Dale* is that the Court felt certain that the BSA, at least, was entitled to expanded protection. If this turns out to be wrong, then the case for expanding the freedom of association into an absolute protection for noncommercial associations becomes weak indeed.

There are three legitimate reasons for the state to forbid discrimination by the BSA. First is the harm to the youth who are subjected to discriminatory treatment — a harm considered in Chapter 5. Perhaps the state cannot prevent this harm — parents have a right to direct the upbringing of their children — but the state can act to ensure that if parents place their children into this potentially toxic environment, they do so with their eyes open. Second, it is doubtful that the BSA's discriminatory policy really does reflect members' preferences better than a regime in which states can prevent discrimination by the BSA within their borders. Finally, there is an interest in ensuring that a major institution of civil society adapts to the cultural norms of the place where it operates. The *Dale* decision has had the perverse effect of damaging the very institution it was trying to protect, driving down the BSA's membership by almost 15 percent. Had the Court remained silent, the BSA would be far better able to perform the precise mediating functions for which the neolibertarians praise the organization. All of these considerations suggest that even if the BSA were within the coverage of the constitutional right to exclude, the interests that conflict with this right may be so compelling as to justify a policy of compelled association, at least in a case like Dale's.

Externalities and Distributive Injustices

The clearest benefit of legal intervention against discrimination is that it will prevent harm to the specific persons who are discriminated against. The harm prevented may outweigh the harm of regulation to the person who is prevented from discriminating. The balance of harms is not determinable by a universal rule in either the economic or the noneconomic sphere.[3] Discrimination has cultural as well as economic externalities: a practice of exclusion that makes insiders very happy may nonetheless injure those who are made pariahs, both because outcast status is bad in itself and because such status is likely to lead to the violation of other rights.[4]

As Chapter 4 argued, unregulated markets often produce unjust distributions. Economics is notoriously indeterminate with respect to initial entitlements. If these are unjust, then a free market will simply perpetuate the injustice: garbage in, garbage out. Similarly with unjustly stigmatized social status. Absent the intervention of the civil rights legislation of the 1960s, America's racism would be worse than it is now. In using coercion to change our culture, we have made ourselves a more just society. The fairness of the distribution of honor and dishonor matters, too.[5]

In the BSA case, the most relevant externalities and distributive injustices concern gay youth. They were the group who most obviously would have benefited from the application of an antidiscrimination statute to the BSA. Chapter 5 noted the stigma with which gay adolescents must cope. If the state is going to combat this prejudice, it cannot be unconcerned with the institutions that promulgate it.

Nan Hunter observes that when entities that generate norms represent themselves as open to the public but then exclude some people on the basis of their identity, that exclusion becomes a marker of inferiority.[6] Some of those entities in fact have enormous norm-generating power, and those norms powerfully stigmatize those who are excluded.[7] If big economic power counts, then so does big power over civil society. As noted earlier, the Boy Scouts of America is now the single largest entity in the United States that excludes gay people on the basis of their identity and justifies this exclusion on the basis of gays' own purported moral failings.

It is possible that these harms do not rise to the level that justifies interference with the BSA's liberty. This was the position of most legislatures before *Dale*. The BSA's cultural power may not be enough to inflict serious harm on many youth. Competition among youth groups and activities may ameliorate the harm of exclusion. But these are fact-dependent questions, the answers to which are likely to vary from place to place. They are not sensibly resolved by a uniform national rule emanating from the courts. The prevention of this kind of mistreatment is not obviously beyond the legitimate power of the state.

The Free Market of Ideas and the Second Best

Thus far, we have been assuming that an unregulated market reflects the preferences of consumers; that if the BSA excludes gays, it is because that is what the members want. The BSA, however, has considerable market power; that market power is reinforced by a kind of government-created monopoly; and as a consequence it is far from clear that regulation must produce a decline in consumer satisfaction.[8]

The position in society of the BSA is not that of one small booth in the pluralist bazaar. It is more like that of Anglicanism in England. The BSA is the largest civic youth organization in the United States, and perhaps in the world. It is deeply intertwined with the state. Since

1916, the BSA has held a congressional charter.[9] It is exempt from a federal statute that bars civilians from wearing uniforms resembling those of the armed forces.[10] Every president since William Howard Taft has been the BSA's honorary president. Congress has authorized the military to loan equipment to the organization without charge and to sell obsolete or surplus material to it.[11] Every four years, the National Jamboree, a huge camping festival that attracts tens of thousands of Scouts from all over the world, is hosted by Fort A. P. Hill in Virginia, a U.S. military base.[12]

Its success in these respects is the result of its calculated decision to present itself as universalistic rather than particularistic. It is pretty late in the day for it now to be presenting itself as one competitor among many.

From the beginning the BSA has emphasized its inclusiveness. One historian of the BSA notes that an important asset was that the organization "adopted a point of view attuned to a democratically minded citizenry and opened its ranks freely to all creeds, races, and classes."[13] Official materials declare that "[n]either [our federal] charter nor the bylaws of the Boy Scouts of America permits the exclusion of any boy."[14] One typical publication urges representatives to give a "[p]ersonal invitation to every boy in school to join scouting."[15] The BSA has declared by its bylaws to be "absolutely nonsectarian."[16] The organization has managed to identify itself with the nation as a whole. "Perhaps the BSA's greatest image-building triumph was its appropriation of the symbols of American nationhood."[17] Bitter differences of religion and ethnicity have been avoided. The history of the BSA with respect to race is less consistently admirable, but even here the organization became inclusive as early as the 1920s, and it was well ahead of the rest of the United States.[18]

Another early success was the monopolization of the term "Boy

Scout." Other organizations used the term when the BSA was founded, but they were eclipsed by the success of the BSA. "[W]ithin its first year of life this organization succeeded in absorbing every other active boy scout group but one — the American Boy Scouts which, though a formidable competitor, also passed from existence before 1920."[19] This triumph was abetted by the congressional charter enacted in 1916, which gave the BSA the exclusive right to use the name of Boy Scouts. This was promptly followed by successful legal action against the competitor organization, which was forced to change its name and did not survive.[20]

After this long history of inclusiveness, the decision of the BSA leadership to plunge into the culture wars betrayed the expectations of much of the membership. The BSA represents social capital built up over many generations, with the active collaboration of the state, in the confidence that the benefits of that entity would be available to all American boys. If the leadership suddenly decides to adopt a policy that alienates a large part of the population, predictably driving hundreds of thousands of youth out of the organization, that need not be a matter of indifference to the government.[21]

The BSA is not a monopoly,[22] but it has enormous market power. The next largest youth organization, Camp Fire USA, has less than a quarter of the BSA's membership.[23] Membership in the BSA has a nationally understood meaning. If you tell someone you are an Eagle Scout, no further explanation is necessary.[24] No other youth organization has such universal recognition or such enormous cultural resonance.[25]

It has been said that those who disagree with the BSA's policies need not be members. If an association is going to develop a coherent voice at all, its internal means of addressing dissent has to be respected by the law.[26] As discussed in Chapter 5, exit is a common method of dissent, and the characteristic means of control in free markets. But as the classic study of the exit option observes, when an organization provides a public good, it is not really possible to exit.[27] One can resign from the BSA, but one must still live in a regime in which the only boys' organization with quasi-official status publicly stands for the proposition that gay people are inherently defective and contaminating. Those who disagree with the BSA leadership's moral judgment — at least a third of the American population — have no comparable option for their children.

Judge Michael McConnell's policy argument for freedom of association analogizes that freedom with freedom of religion, as noted in Chapter 4. The analogy is problematic because no religion in the United States represents an overwhelming majority of the pertinent population in the way that the BSA does. If we put some pressure on the analogy, we will see the important ways in which freedom of association is legally constrained, to the benefit of the BSA, even after *Dale*.

In a regime of free association like that which has prevailed in the religion area, the BSA would face a real possibility of schism over the homosexuality issue.[28] In February 2001, the New York City board of the BSA declared that the national organization's ban on gays was "repugnant" and "stupid."[29] New York's leadership later joined with those of Chicago, Los Angeles, San Francisco, Philadelphia, Minneapolis, and Orange County, California, in proposing that the ban be discarded.[30] Yet none of these cities' councils has officially rejected the national policy. The national organization has too much leverage over them for them to do that. Philadelphia's council tried to adopt a nondiscrimination policy in May 2003 but quickly reversed itself after the national organization threatened to revoke the council's charter.[31] One member reported, "They told us essentially that unless you issue a statement saying you will adhere specifically and literally to the national discriminatory standard, we will pull your charter, we'll close your camps, and, essentially, we'll shut down Scouting for 65,000 kids in the Philadelphia area."[32]

American churches have divided in the past over fundamental moral differences. When northern and southern churches disagreed about slavery, the Presbyterians, Methodists, and Baptists each split into separate regional churches.[33] Similarly today, there is a serious danger of division over the moral status of homosexual conduct among Presbyterians, Lutherans, Episcopalians, and Methodists.[34]

When these religious splits have occurred, the state has remained neutral. After the rift over slavery, the respective factions on both sides of the Mason-Dixon line continued to call themselves Presbyterians, Methodists, and Baptists and to follow the rituals of their respective denominations. Neither side attempted to enjoin these practices by the other. More recently, the Society of St. Pius X is a group of Catholics who are in schism from the Catholic Church, their leaders excommunicated by the Pope, because of their rejection of the Vatican II reforms.[35] A number of churches of the society operate in the United States, and it has hundreds of members here.[36] During the schism, they celebrated the Catholic Mass using the priestly clothing and language traditionally associated with the church. No effort was ever made by the church to claim that these rituals and symbols were its intellectual property, or to legally enjoin the society from operating as it did.

The law of intellectual property is, however, a potentially powerful instrument for crushing religious diversity. Religious groups are protected as much as other groups from competitors with similar names, on principles analogous to those applied in trademark and trade name cases.[37] Present law might well have authorized the Pope to enjoin

Martin Luther from calling himself a "Christian." What has kept this rule from being a disaster for American religious pluralism is that few religious denominations have tried to enjoin each other from existing,[38] and nothing of this sort happened in the major divisions just noted.

There is, however, every reason to think that the BSA leadership would use the law to suppress any schism within its ranks. Any troop that separated from the BSA would have to give up its uniforms and its curriculum.[39] It would have to alter itself in a fundamental way. If it attempted to continue while disavowing the antigay policy, the BSA would presumably get an injunction to force it to stop identifying itself as a Boy Scout troop.

What the BSA leadership has after *Dale* is the best of both worlds: freedom of association protects their right to discriminate, but their congressional charter and intellectual property law prevent dissenting factions, even those with tens of thousands of members, from splitting off. If the religion analogy is accepted, then it should be pushed to its limits and the BSA exposed to the dangers of schism that American religions routinely cope with.[40] Of course, the Supreme Court, having decided to protect the BSA in *Dale,* could not then order that its intellectual property protections be lifted. The Court has no authority to do so. But this is one more reason why these matters should have been left to legislatures, which have the flexibility to craft solutions of this kind.

The present regime does not unproblematically reflect the preferences of local associations.[41] The application of antidiscrimination law would be a great relief to some local councils, who after *Dale* are squeezed between their own, gay-tolerant moral beliefs (and those of their donors and members) and the national policy. The antigay policy has become a powerful obstacle to fundraising and the recruitment of volunteers in precisely those urban areas where the benefits of Scouting are most urgently needed. It is in such areas that volunteers and money are especially scarce, and troops depend upon corporate donations supporting paid staff.[42] "There are probably a hundred positive things that Scouting affords young people," commented Lewis Greenblatt, then president of the Chicago Area Council of the BSA, in 2002. "This is one of the few negative things that is going on in Scouting. In Chicago, our core group is kids from the inner city. Scouting offers them some extremely positive reinforcement that they don't otherwise get." Chicago's council has expressed its disagreement with the national policy, but it is not openly repudiating it. "We've gone about as far as we can go. We're right up to the line," Greenblatt said.[43]

The Chicago council would be greatly strengthened in its negotiations with national headquarters if the Chicago human rights ordinance could constitutionally be applied to it. It could tell headquarters that it had no choice but to comply, while telling locals forthrightly that it doesn't discriminate.[44] The council could then do its local work with the homosexuality issue firmly off the table. The controversy over antigay discrimination, which the Chicago council did not invite, would disappear. The *Dale* decision has made it impossible for the issue to be resolved in this way.

Instead, all over the country, the BSA is being stigmatized as a discriminatory organization. Charitable contributions are down, and so is membership. Many municipalities that previously provided meeting and park space to the BSA for free are now declining to do so because the organization discriminates. This has produced bitterness on both sides, with the BSA leadership and the cities each blaming the other for inflexibility. Both sides are, of course, standing up for principles that they believe in. Each finds the other's principles repugnant.

But they cannot escape from one another because the Supreme Court has forced a national solution to what should be a set of local problems.

Concerns have been raised that, had *Dale* come out the other way, the BSA would have suffered a different kind of damage. The BSA's largest religious sponsors threatened to abandon the organization if it were forced to admit gays.[45] But it is most doubtful that these groups would have done so nationally. Whatever social capital they would have lost seems dwarfed by the losses sustained in the aftermath of *Dale*. Moreover, substitutes for the BSA are more attractive in some places than others, and the regions most resistant to a nondiscrimination rule are probably the ones that can most easily do without the BSA. If, for instance, the BSA disappeared from Salt Lake City tomorrow, other groups would recruit the Mormon boys without much strain. Compare the rival groups, mainly violent drug-dealing gangs, that are eager to recruit boys in the inner cities of Chicago and Philadelphia.

The BSA would doubtless respond that any loss of membership is a cost worth bearing for the sake of the principle it is upholding. This may make sense for the organization, but it cannot for their scholarly defenders who are eager to support a vibrant civil society that mediates between the individual and the state. From that standpoint, the shrinkage of the BSA has to count as a devastating loss — all the more so because it is likely most pronounced where Scouting is most needed.

Dale then is, in the ways that matter most, a defeat rather than a victory for pluralism. The pluralist argument for an absolute freedom of association depends on a simplistic, binary view of the constraints on association, in which associations are either subject to state power or absolutely free to organize themselves as they see fit. In fact, as the Chicago case shows, associations actually operate in a complex web of constraints, including the state, their umbrella organizations, and various groups of constituents, including donors, volunteers, and members. Eliminating state control does not always increase a local association's ability to reflect the preferences of its members. In many of the nation's largest cities, the opposite has been the case. Local BSA troops *are* bullied by a distant bureaucracy; that bureaucracy just happens to be a nonstate entity.

The libertarianism of *Dale* is analogous to that of *United States v. E. C. Knight Co.,*[46] the 1895 case which held that Congress had no power to regulate a trust that controlled 98 percent of the country's sugar refining industry. The Supreme Court's disabling of government power did not empower anybody except the monopolists who controlled the trust. Similarly here, the Court's constraint on public power produces a hypertrophy of private power. Judge McConnell would read the religion clauses to "protect against government-induced uniformity in matters of religion,"[47] and his argument for freedom of association suggests similar concerns. Yet the *Dale* case has itself induced uniformity. Had the case come out the other way, the result would be different in different states.

Even in Chicago, some local troops would probably have wanted to continue to discriminate. They could have done so even before *Dale.* As the BSA's brief in *Dale* noted, expressive association (which is what this book has focused on) was not the only issue raised by the BSA's policy; there were also issues of intimate association and parental control over children's upbringing that might be constitutionally relevant (though, as the Court evidently noticed, they were not going to help the BSA in Dale's case).[48] It is unlikely that there would ever be a single rule for the entire nation. This proliferation of options is one of the traditional strengths of federalism.[49]

The problem in the *Dale* case thus resembles that described in what economists call the "theory of the second best."[50] The theory holds that when many markets are not competitive, it may be counterefficient to attack monopolies in only some segments of the market. Consumers may respond to the regulation by shifting to unregulated activities that are even more inefficient than the activities that regulation drove them away from, resulting in a net efficiency loss.

Here, if the BSA possesses a quasi-monopoly over a valuable cultural resource, freeing the organization from state regulation will not improve the market. It may just produce still greater consumer dissatisfaction. If the first best solution of free association isn't available, a message-based approach may be the second best.

Conclusion

The most powerful claim of the BSA, stated in its brief before the U.S. Supreme Court, was that "American pluralism thrives on difference"[51] and that "controversial questions of personal morality, often involving religious conviction, are best tested and resolved within the private marketplace of ideas, and not as the subject of government-imposed orthodoxy."[52]

Pluralism is valuable. So is the autonomy of diverse groups. But it doesn't follow that these values should always take priority over the effort to break up entrenched patterns of discrimination and include, in socially valued activities, people who have traditionally been outcasts.[53] The harms of discrimination are particularly acute for children; gay youth suffer severe developmental harm when forced to lie and hide their identities, which is precisely what the BSA's policy requires of the millions of gay adolescents who discover their sexuality when they are already members. The prevention of such harm is not a trivial state interest.

The question of the state's interest in *Dale* is really two questions, one normative and one empirical. The normative question is whether discrimination against gays is a bad thing. Here, public opinion is rapidly shifting. Discrimination against gays may once have seemed the neutral and normal thing to do; it may still seem that way to some. It would, however, be an abuse of judicial power for the Court to read that view into the Constitution and so to disable legislatures from addressing what is increasingly understood as a severe problem. If there ever were a cultural moment when the Court should be neutral on the question of the morality of homosexual conduct, this is it.[54]

The empirical question is whether laws like New Jersey's are necessary to remedy gays' outcast status. This question cannot be answered from the judicial (or the academic!) armchair, insulated from experience. Perhaps the autonomy of groups like the BSA does not pose much of a threat to the equality of gays. Perhaps competition among groups will provide a satisfactory remedy for any pattern of exclusion. But such imponderables are poor candidates for sweeping constitutional rules. The Court's awareness of its limitations is commendable but did not go far enough.

The big question is the scope of legitimate state interests. The neolibertarian argument works only if the state does not have legitimate interests that would be impaired by an absolute right to discriminate. If there are such interests, then the absolute right to discriminate is too crude a rule, disabling the state from addressing real harms.

The Supreme Court has become more and more oblivious to the legitimate reasons for regulating associations. If, however, courts cannot trust themselves to judge associations' messages, yet there are legitimate reasons for regulation, what follows is not absolute protection, but judicial deference. If there is not to be deference, then there is no alternative to balancing.

These cases illustrate a more general point. Even if a sphere of society works best if it is mostly unregulated, this does not settle the question of whether any particular regulation is appropriate. The situation with respect to noncommercial associations is much like that with respect to businesses. A free market is a good thing, and capitalist economies generate enormous wealth. The case for or against any particular regulation must nonetheless be made at retail.[55] Efforts to produce more general rules produce astounding pathologies.

Notes

Introduction

1. Chuck Sudetic, *The Struggle for the Soul of the Boy Scouts,* Rolling Stone, July 6–20, 2000, at 105.
2. *Id.*
3. 530 U.S. 640 (2000).
4. 547 U.S. 47 (2006).
5. For the most part, membership in Scouting is confined to boys, but one program, Venturing, is open to older girls. See http://www.scouting .org/venturing.aspx (visited Sept. 16, 2008).

Chapter 1. Origins of the Right to Exclude

1. There is a very good literature on the effect of the regulation of association upon the right of free speech, notably the extensive treatment in Harry Kalven Jr., A Worthy Tradition: Free Speech in America 241–587 (Jamie Kalven ed., 1988), but it does not focus on the right to exclude.
2. The linkage to Kant is clearest in Robert Nozick, Anarchy, State, and Utopia (1974).

3. A modern proponent of this view is Michael Levin, *Negative Liberty*, 2 Soc. Phil. & Pol'y 84, 98–100 (1984). This type of argument is applied specifically to the BSA case in Roy Whitehead Jr. and Walter Block, *The Boy Scouts, Freedom of Association, and the Right to Discriminate: A Legal, Philosophical, and Economic Analysis*, 29 Okla. City L. Rev. 851 (2004). George Kateb approaches the position described in the text but shrinks from it without much explanation, conceding that businesses, at least, may legitimately be denied the right to discriminate. George Kateb, *The Value of Association*, in Freedom of Association 35, 58 (Amy Gutmann ed., 1998).

4. See Charles Taylor, *Atomism*, in Philosophy and the Human Sciences: Philosophical Papers 2 187 (1985).

5. See Thomas W. Pogge, Realizing Rawls 15–62 (1989).

6. See Andrew Koppelman, Antidiscrimination Law and Social Equality 43–47, 181–90 (1996).

7. See Samuel Freeman, *Illiberal Libertarians: Why Libertarianism Is Not a Liberal View*, 30 Phil. & Pub. Aff. 105 (2001).

8. See Allen D. Rosen, Kant's Theory of Justice 173–208 (1993). Nozick, the most prominent exponent of this type of libertarianism, eventually recanted. See Robert Nozick, The Examined Life 286–96 (1989).

9. Both claims are prominent in, for example, Friedrich A. Hayek, The Road to Serfdom (1944); Friedrich A. Hayek, Law, Legislation, and Liberty, v. 2: The Mirage of Social Justice (1976).

10. See Ian Shapiro, The Evolution of Rights in Liberal Theory 80–203 (1986). Alternately, one can argue, as the early libertarian Herbert Spencer did, that unregulated markets will produce misery and starvation, but that this is a good thing because it tends to weed out the unfit. See Samuel Fleischacker, A Short History of Distributive Justice 86–94 (2004).

11. The classic argument is John Rawls, A Theory of Justice (1971).

12. Steven P. Croley, *Public Interested Regulation*, 28 Fla. St. L. Rev. 7 (2000).

13. See Lisa Heinzerling, *Regulatory Costs of Mythic Proportions*, 107 Yale L.J. 1981 (1998).

14. Richard A. Epstein, Forbidden Grounds: The Case against Employment Discrimination Laws (1992). That his basic philosophical orientation is consequentialist rather than rights-based is made clear in Richard Epstein, *Standing Firm, on Forbidden Grounds*, 31 San Diego L. Rev. 1 (1994).

15. See Glenn C. Loury, *Why Should We Care about Group Inequality?*, 5 Soc. Phil. & Pol'y 249, 253–59 (Aut. 1987); David Strauss, *The Law and Economics of Racial Discrimination in Employment: The Case for Numerical Standards,* 79 Georgetown L.J. 1619 (1991); Cass R. Sunstein, *Why Markets Don't Stop Discrimination,* 8 Soc. Phil. & Pol'y 22 (Spr. 1991). The weaknesses of Epstein's attack on antidiscrimination laws are canvassed in detail in a symposium at 31 San Diego L. Rev. 1–277 (1994), and in Samuel Issacharoff, *Contractual Liberties in Discriminatory Markets,* 70 Tex. L. Rev. 1219 (1992) (review of Forbidden Grounds). Epstein's view also rests on the dubious argument that malign ideologies such as racism have no effect on anyone's life chances, and so the state ought to ignore them. See Epstein, Forbidden Grounds, at 498–99; Koppelman, Antidiscrimination Law and Social Equality, at 118–19.

16. James J. Heckman and J. Hoult Verkerke, *Racial Disparity and Employment Discrimination Law: An Economic Perspective,* 8 Yale L. & Pol'y Rev. 276 (1990).

17. Ronald Dworkin, *Equality of Resources,* in Sovereign Virtue: The Theory and Practice of Equality 65 (2000).

18. Hayek, The Mirage of Social Justice, at 30.

19. The following discussion is deeply indebted to Joseph William Singer, *No Right to Exclude: Public Accommodations and Private Property,* 90 Nw. U. L. Rev. 1283 (1996).

20. *Id.* at 1344.

21. *Id.* at 1321–31. This rule is expressly followed today in some jurisdictions. See, e.g., *Uston v. Resorts Int'l Hotel,* 445 A.2d 370 (N.J. 1982).

22. Singer at 1323 n.149; *Beall v. Beck,* 2 F.Cas. 1111, 1116 (C.C.D.C. 1829).

23. Singer at 1331–45, 1348–73.

24. *Bowlin v. Lyon,* 25 N.W. 766, 767 (Iowa 1885), quoted in Singer at 1391. The same court declared in 1909 that it is "the right of a trader whose business is purely of private character to trade with whom he will, and he may discriminate as he pleases," so that the trader "may exclude all working men, all colored people, all Irishmen, all Jews, or all Adventists for reasons which seem to him sufficient. These reasons may be based upon either race or religious prejudice, and yet the court would not be justified in saying that any right had been invaded." *Brown v. J. H. Bell Co.,* 123 N.W. 231, 233, 236 (Iowa 1909), quoted in Singer at 1402–03.

25. *State v. Steele,* 11 S.E. 478, 484 (N.C. 1890), quoted in Singer at 1388.

"Although the narrowing of public accommodations law appears, on the surface, to cohere with emerging protections for property owners, the inconsistency between property rights as conceived in this period and Jim Crow statutes suggests that changes in public accommodations law are far more tied to racial politics than to laissez-faire philosophy or the protection of property from government regulation." Singer at 1395.

26. Singer at 1295.

27. The tension between strong property rights and compulsory segregation is noted in Singer at 1295 n.32, 1388–1390.

28. *West Chester & Philadelphia R.R. v. Miles*, 55 Pa. 209, 212–13 (1867).

29. *Id.* at 213–14. Other, similar statements by nineteenth-century courts are collected in Reva Siegel, *Why Equal Protection No Longer Protects: The Evolving Forms of Status-Enforcing State Action*, 49 Stan. L. Rev. 1111, 1123–27 (1997).

30. *Plessy v. Ferguson*, 163 U.S. 537, 551 (1896).

31. C. Vann Woodward, The Strange Career of Jim Crow 104–05 (3d rev. ed. 1974).

32. See, e.g., David E. Bernstein, *The Story of* Lochner v. New York: *Impediment to the Growth of the Regulatory State*, in Constitutional Law Stories 325 (Michael C. Dorf ed., 2004).

33. See William Novak, The People's Welfare: Law and Regulation in Nineteenth-Century America 186–88 (1996), discussing *Wynehamer v. People*, 13 N.Y. 378 (1856).

34. 198 U.S. 45 (1905).

35. Davison M. Douglas, *Contract Rights and Civil Rights*, 100 Mich. L. Rev. 1541, 1555–56 (2002).

36. See, e.g., *Pickett v. Kuchan*, 153 N.E. 667 (Ill. 1926); *Greeneberg v. Western Turf Ass'n*, 73 P. 1050 (Calif. 1903); *People v. King*, 18 N.E. 245 (N.Y. 1888); *Joseph v. Bidwell*, 28 La. Ann. 382 (1876); *Donnell v. State*, 48 Miss. 661 (1873).

37. 48 Miss. 661 (1873).

38. *Id.* at 663.

39. *Id.* at 664.

40. *Id.* at 681.

41. *People v. King*, 18 N.E. 245, 248 (N.Y. 1888).

42. Douglas, *Contract Rights and Civil Rights*, at 1555–59.

43. 211 U.S. 45 (1908).

44. *Id.* at 54.
45. *Id.* at 69 (Harlan, J., dissenting). The lower court, on the other hand, had indicated that voluntary association of students was precisely what the state had an overriding interest in preventing, since it could lead to inter-marriage. *Berea College v. Commonwealth*, 94 S.W. 623 (Ky. App. 1906).
46. *Buchanan v. Warley*, 245 U.S. 60 (1917).
47. *Meyer v. Nebraska*, 262 U.S. 390 (1923). See also *Farrington v. Tokushige*, 273 U.S. 284 (1927), striking down the Territory of Hawaii's law barring the teaching of foreign languages without a permit.
48. *Pierce v. Society of Sisters*, 268 U.S. 510 (1925).
49. 326 U.S. 88 (1945).
50. Brief of Appellants at 32–33, *Corsi.*
51. *Corsi*, 326 U.S. at 93–94.
52. *Id.*
53. *Steele v. Louisville & N.R. Co.*, 323 U.S. 192 (1944); *Tunstall v. Brotherhood of Locomotive Firemen*, 323 U.S. 210 (1944). See generally Risa Goluboff, The Lost Promise of Civil Rights (2007). The same duty of fair representation has since been read into the National Labor Relations Act. *Syres v. Oil Workers, Local 23*, 350 U.S. 892 (1955).
54. Goluboff at 37.
55. *James v. Marinship Corp.*, 155 P.2d 329, 338 (Calif. 1945).
56. *Id.* at 335. Later cases applied the same standard to unions without local monopolies. Goluboff at 206.
57. Goluboff at 205.
58. A good brief history of the White Primary cases is Samuel Issacharoff and Richard H. Pildes, *Politics as Markets: Partisan Lockups of the Democratic Process,* 50 Stan. L. Rev. 643, 652–58 (1998).
59. 321 U.S. 649 (1944).
60. Brief of George A. Butler, Chairman of State Democratic Executive Committee of Texas, as Amicus Curiae, *Smith v. Allwright*, 321 U.S. 649 (1944), at 5.
61. Brief of Gerald C. Mann, Attorney General of Texas, as Amicus Curiae, *Smith v. Allwright*, 321 U.S. 649 (1944), at 3; see also *id.* at 10, 14 (citing First Amendment). The same argument had been accepted by the Supreme Court of Texas. *Bell v. Hill*, 47 S.W.2d 113, 120 (Tex. 1934), quoted in *Smith*, 321 U.S. at 654–56.
62. *Smith*, 321 U.S. at 663.

63. 345 U.S. 461 (1953).

64. Brief for Respondents, *Terry v. Adams*, 345 U.S. 461 (1953), at 41.

65. *Terry*, 345 U.S. at 493–94 (Minton, J., dissenting).

66. The weak formalism of the decision is noted in Issacharoff and Pildes at 659–60.

67. Brief of Attorney General at 26–27.

68. 347 U.S. 483 (1954).

69. Herbert Wechsler, *Toward Neutral Principles of Constitutional Law,* 73 Harv. L. Rev. 1, 34 (1959).

70. Charles L. Black Jr., *The Lawfulness of the Segregation Decisions,* 69 Yale L.J. 421, 429 (1960).

71. Rick Perlstein, Before the Storm: Barry Goldwater and the Unmaking of the American Consensus 363–64 (2001) (Rehnquist and Bork advised Goldwater that the act was unconstitutional on this basis); *id.* at 462 (quoting Goldwater speech, coauthored by Rehnquist and political theorist Harry Jaffa, declaring that "the freedom to associate means the same thing as the freedom not to associate"); Ayn Rand, The Virtue of Selfishness: A New Concept of Egoism 126–34 (1964); Robert Bork, *Civil Rights—A Challenge,* 149 New Republic, Aug. 31, 1963, at 22. See also Barry Goldwater, The Conscience of a Conservative 33–37 (1960) (rejecting *Brown v. Board of Education* on states' rights grounds, and proposing that it be overruled by constitutional amendment). The idea that antidiscrimination laws should not be applied to the private sector had earlier been endorsed by some prominent liberals, such as Oswald Garrison Villard and Hannah Arendt. David E. Bernstein, You Can't Say That! The Growing Threat to Civil Liberties from Antidiscrimination Laws 5 (2003).

72. *Heart of Atlanta Motel, Inc. v. United States*, 379 U.S. 241, 258–61 (1964).

73. 357 U.S. 449 (1958) (Harlan, J.).

74. *Id.* at 462.

75. *Id.* at 460.

76. *Id.* at 463–66.

77. 427 U.S. 160 (1976).

78. *Id.* at 176.

79. *Id.*, quoting *McCrary v. Runyon*, 515 F.2d 1082, 1087 (4th Cir. 1975).

80. 468 U.S. 609 (1984). As noted above, it was argued, but ignored by the Court, in *Smith v. Allwright*.

81. *Id.* at 623.

82. *Id.* (emphasis added).

83. In one of the key passages, the Court explained:

> While acknowledging that "the specific content of most of the resolutions adopted over the years by the Jaycees has nothing to do with sex," the Court of Appeals nonetheless entertained the hypothesis that women members might have a different view or agenda with respect to these matters so that, if they are allowed to vote, "some change in the Jaycees' philosophical cast can reasonably be expected." It is similarly arguable that, insofar as the Jaycees is organized to promote the views of young men whatever those views happen to be, admission of women as voting members will change the message communicated by the group's speech because of the gender-based assumptions of the audience. Neither supposition, however, is supported by the record.

Id. at 627–28.

84. At least one court has issued such a holding in a related situation. In *Invisible Empire of the Knights of the Ku Klux Klan v. Mayor et al. of Thurmont*, 700 F. Supp. 281, 289–91 (D. Md. 1988), a district court found that the KKK could not be denied a permit to march on a town's public streets because of the group's objection to a demand by the mayor that they comply with a nondiscrimination condition in their choice of whom to include as marchers. (No issue of membership in the KKK chapter itself was presented.) From the discussion in the opinion, it appears that black and Jewish protestors would have marched with the KKK, if allowed, in order to spoil their message. *Id.* at 289. Prefiguring the result in *Hurley,* the district court essentially treated the KKK's choice of whom to include in a parade as a question of pure expression and invalidated the attempt to mandate the inclusion of unwanted members. *Id.* at 290–91. See *Hurley v. Irish-American Gay, Lesbian & Bisexual Group of Boston*, 515 U.S. 557 (1995) (holding that a private parade organizer has a First Amendment right to exercise control over the groups that will march under their own banners in the parade, as that feature of the parade's composition itself constitutes protected expression).

85. *Roberts*, 468 U.S. at 623.

86. See *Board of Dirs. of Rotary Int'l v. Rotary Club of Duarte*, 481 U.S. 537 (1987); *New York State Club Ass'n v. City of New York*, 487 U.S. 1 (1988).

87. *Eu v. San Francisco Democratic Cent. Comm.*, 489 U.S. 214 (1989); *Tashijian v. Republican Party*, 479 U.S. 208 (1986); *Democratic Party of United States v. Wisconsin ex rel. LaFollette*, 450 U.S. 107 (1981).

88. See, e.g., *Scales v. United States*, 367 U.S. 203 (1961).

89. See *Freedom of Assembly and Association*, in Encyclopedia of the American Constitution 1106–07 (2d ed. 2000).

90. See Cass R. Sunstein, Democracy and the Problem of Free Speech (1993); Harry Kalven Jr., *The New York Times Case: A Note on "The Central Meaning of the First Amendment,"* 1964 Sup. Ct. Rev. 191; Alexander Meiklejohn, Political Freedom (1960).

91. See John Stuart Mill, On Liberty (1859).

92. See David A. Strauss, *Persuasion, Autonomy, and Freedom of Expression*, 91 Colum. L. Rev. 334 (1991); Martin Redish, Freedom of Expression: A Critical Analysis (1984); C. Edwin Baker, *The Scope of the First Amendment Freedom of Speech*, 25 U.C.L.A. L. Rev. 964 (1978); David A. J. Richards, *Free Speech and Obscenity Law: Toward a Moral Theory of the First Amendment*, 123 U. Pa. L. Rev. 45 (1974); T. M. Scanlon, *A Theory of Freedom of Expression*, 1 Phil. & Pub. Aff. 204 (1972).

93. *Roberts*, 468 U.S. at 622.

94. Robert C. Post and Nancy L. Rosenblum, *Introduction*, in Civil Society and Government 17–19 (2002).

95. *Roberts*, 468 U.S. at 622.

96. *Id.* at 627.

Chapter 2. Signs of the Times

1. 530 U.S. 640 (2000).

2. Quoted in *id.* at 643.

3. *Boy Scouts of America v. Dale*, 160 N.J. 562, 613, 734 A.2d 1196, 1223–24 (1999) (internal quotation marks omitted), quoted in *Dale*, 530 U.S. at 647.

4. 160 N.J. at 615, 734 A.2d at 1225, quoting *Board of Directors of Rotary Int'l v. Rotary Club of Duarte*, 481 U.S. 537, 548 (1987); quoted in *Dale*, 530 U.S. at 647.

5. *Dale*, 530 U.S. at 650.

6. *Id.*

7. *Id.* at 653.

8. *Id.*

9. *Id.* at 655. In an earlier opinion, the Court had taken a narrower view, declaring that "[i]t is possible to find some kernel of expression in almost every activity a person undertakes—for example, walking down the street or meeting one's friends at a shopping mall—but such a kernel is not sufficient to bring the activity within the protection of the First Amendment." *City of Dallas v. Stanglin*, 490 U.S. 19, 25 (1989).

10. See Richard Epstein, *The Constitutional Perils of Moderation: The Case of the Boy Scouts*, 74 S. Cal. L. Rev. 119, 139–40 (2000); Jed Rubenfeld, *The First Amendment's Purpose*, 53 Stan. L. Rev. 767, 812 (2001).

11. Quoted in Brief for Respondent, *Boy Scouts of America v. Dale*, 2000 WL 340276, at 3. In the years immediately after the litigation, the BSA was much more forthright about its policy on its Web page, http://www .scouting.org. When I visited the page again in early 2008, all discussion of the gay exclusion had disappeared, and a list of press releases showed that there had not been a single press release addressing the issue since 2006. However, the issue is discussed at an official BSA Website concerning legal issues, http://www.bsalegal.org.

12. *Dale,* 530 U.S. at 651. The dangers of judicial scrutiny of an association's purposes are considered in more detail in Chapter 4.

13. See *Katzenbach v. McClung*, 379 U.S. 294 (1964).

14. The restaurant was still in existence when *Dale* was decided. It closed in 2001. See *Ollie's BBQ Closes, but the Sauce Will Live On*, Birmingham Business Journal, Sept. 21, 2001, http://www.bizjournals.com/birming ham/stories/2001/09/24/tidbits.html (visited Oct. 10, 2007).

15. At one point, the Court does note that "[t]he Boy Scouts is a private, nonprofit organization," 530 U.S. at 649, but it does not state that this fact has any legal significance.

16. *Id.* at 695 (Stevens, J., dissenting).

17. *Id.* at 702 (Souter, J., dissenting).

18. *Id.* at 653 (majority opinion).

19. See Rick Perlstein, Before the Storm: Barry Goldwater and the Unmaking of the American Consensus 363 (2001).

20. See Epstein, *The Constitutional Perils of Moderation*, at 139; Richard Epstein, *Free Association: The Incoherence of Antidiscrimination Laws,* National

Review, Oct. 9, 2000. On the other hand, it was possible that he was prepared to invalidate — on states' rights rather than free association grounds — some applications of that same civil rights statute to the states. See Robert Post and Reva Siegel, *Equal Protection by Law: Federal Antidiscrimination Legislation After* Morrison *and* Kimel, 110 Yale L.J. 441, 452 (2000).

21. *Roberts v. United States Jaycees*, 468 U.S. 609, 633–34 (1984) (O'Connor, J., concurring in part and concurring in the judgment).

22. *Id.* at 635.

23. *Id.* at 636.

24. During the oral argument in *Dale,* Justice O'Connor asked whether the case might be resolved by relying on the commercial/noncommercial distinction. *Boy Scouts of America v. Dale*, transcript of oral argument, 2000 WL 489419, at 23.

25. Daniel A. Farber, *Speaking in the First Person Plural: Expressive Associations and the First Amendment,* 85 Minn. L. Rev. 1483, 1500 (2001). Justice O'Connor had written that a commercial association is not protected even if it engages in expressive activity. See *Roberts,* 468 U.S. at 639 (O'Connor, J., concurring in part and concurring in the judgment); *New York State Club Ass'n v. City of New York*, 487 U.S. 1, 20 (1988) (O'Connor, J., joined by Kennedy, J., concurring).

26. As does David Bernstein, *Antidiscrimination Laws and the First Amendment,* 66 Mo. L. Rev. 83, 126–27 (2001); David Bernstein, *The Right of Expressive Association and Private Universities' Racial Preferences and Speech Codes,* 9 Wm. & Mary Bill of Rts. J. 619, 626 (2001).

27. As does Dale Carpenter in his otherwise fine elaboration of O'Connor's theory. See Dale Carpenter, *Expressive Association and Anti-Discrimination Law after* Dale: *A Tripartite Approach,* 85 Minn. L. Rev. 1515 (2001).

28. David McGowan has correctly observed that this fact cuts against the reading offered in this section: "reading the Court as holding that Dale's homosexuality was inherently expressive would make large portions of the opinion irrelevant." David McGowan, *Making Sense of* Dale, 18 Const. Comm. 121, 140 (2001). There is, however, no reading of *Dale* that can coherently account for all of its parts and fit them into a plausible decision. Even if, as McGowan thinks, the idea that Dale's status as inherently a message-bearer stemmed from his status as a "gay rights activist," see *id.,* this status, if legally relevant, would still render most of the opinion

irrelevant. Moreover, McGowan's view that "the question whether the Scouts would have a speech-based right to exclude a gay man who was not an activist is left unresolved," *id.*, seems unduly optimistic. Dale was not expelled for being an activist, but for being gay. One of the things that defined him as an "activist" in the Court's opinion was the fact that he was "open and honest about [his] sexual orientation." *Dale,* 530 U.S. at 653. The Court may well have perceived Dale as "fairly shouting a message on a topic the Scouts wanted to avoid," McGowan at 172, but this is a strange characterization of Dale's own speech. See the description of the news article that triggered his expulsion, below.

29. *Dale,* 530 U.S. at 653.

30. 515 U.S. 557 (1995).

31. 530 U.S. at 654. Jed Rubenfeld's analysis of *Dale* comes close to mine, but he reads the case differently than I do, as holding that "people are constitutionally entitled to violate a conduct law of general applicability because they have important expressive reasons for doing so." Rubenfeld, *The First Amendment's Purpose,* at 817. The passages just quoted, however, show that *Dale* rests on a finding of compelled speech. Compelled speech is distinct from, and constitutionally worse than, "prohibit[ing] some persons from expressing opinions or values in the way they want to express them." *Id.* at 809. The difference matters because, under existing case law, the prohibition on compelled speech seems to be an absolute that transcends the balancing that (in the remainder of his article) Rubenfeld deplores. If obedience to a law of general applicability is compelled speech, then government can't require it even if the costs of disobedience outweigh the benefits. *Dale* is thus even crazier than Rubenfeld thinks it is.

32. *West Virginia Board of Education v. Barnette,* 319 U.S. 624, 634 (1943).

33. *Glickman v. Wileman Brothers & Elliott,* 521 U.S. 457, 471 (1997).

34. See, e.g., *United States v. United Foods,* 533 U.S. 405, 410–11 (2001). The prohibition on compelled speech applies with undiminished force to commercial speech and speech by corporations. See *id.*; *Pacific Gas v. Public Util. Comm'n,* 475 U.S. 1 (1986).

35. *Dale,* 530 U.S. at 653, citations omitted.

36. See also *Dale,* 530 U.S. at 655–56 ("The presence of an avowed homosexual and gay rights activist in an assistant scoutmaster's uniform sends a distinctly different message from the presence of a heterosexual assistant scoutmaster who is on record as disagreeing with Boy Scouts policy. The

Boy Scouts has a First Amendment right to choose to send one message but not the other.").

37. *Seminar addresses needs of homosexual teens,* Star Ledger, July 8, 1990, quoted in *Dale,* 530 U.S. at 689–90 (Stevens, J., dissenting).

38. Professor Wolff finds the seeds of this argument in *Hurley* itself. In analyzing the compelled speech claim in the context of an inherently expressive parade, the *Hurley* Court explained that "openly" gay men and lesbians were free to march in the Boston St. Patrick's Day parade and that it was only GLIB's insistence that it be allowed to march under its own banner that implicated the First Amendment. *See Hurley,* 515 U.S. 557, 572 (1995). But, as Professor Wolff explains, this distinction offers little reassurance when examined more carefully:

> While seemingly attractive as a means of downplaying the intolerance of the Council's position, . . . the space that this distinction carves out is a very small one, indeed. What could the Court mean, after all, when it suggests that the participation of "openly" gay, lesbian or bisexual people was not contested in *Hurley*? Does it mean for "open" to refer only to the perceptions of other marchers, suggesting that gay men and lesbians remained "free," for example, to discuss their same-sex spouses with other parade participants, but only so long as they were not otherwise identifiable as gay and marched anonymously in the parade? Within the context of the Court's analysis, this constrained reading is necessary in order to make any sense of the assertion that "open" gay men and lesbians were free to march. The Court could not have meant "open" to refer to the perceptions of the parade's audience, for it would run directly contrary to the logic of the opinion to allow the State to require the participation of this latter kind of "openly gay" individual while forbidding the State to mandate the inclusion of GLIB.
>
> If any individual marcher in the parade were identifiably gay — if he held hands with his same-sex partner, for example, or if he were a famous public figure who was widely known to be gay because he had come out of the closet on national television — then the presence of that individual would as much "bear witness to the fact that some Irish are gay, lesbian or bisexual" as would a GLIB parade unit. . . . The Court's opinion in *Hurley* rests on the under-

standing that whenever an identity is perceived to be present—whether that identity is implicit, like the presumed heterosexuality of the marchers in the Boston parade, or explicit, like a hypothetical Irish counterpart to Ellen DeGeneres or Congressman Barney Frank—the identity constitutes meaningful and intelligible speech.

Tobias Barrington Wolff, *Compelled Affirmations, Free Speech, and the U.S. Military's Don't Ask, Don't Tell Policy,* 63 Brook. L. Rev. 1141, 1191 n.150 (1997).

39. "The right to control its own message includes the organization's right to be silent about issues if it so chooses. Boy Scouting does not convey an explicit 'anti-gay' message to the boys under its care; but it does not wish to convey approval of homosexual conduct either." Brief for Petitioner at 21.

40. Arthur S. Leonard, Boy Scouts of America v. Dale: *The "Gay Rights Activist" as Constitutional Pariah,* 12 Stanford L. & Pol'y Rev. 27, 27 (2001). See also *Dale,* 530 U.S. at 696 (Stevens, J., dissenting):

> Under the majority's reasoning, an openly gay male is irreversibly affixed with the label "homosexual." That label, even though unseen, communicates a message that permits his exclusion wherever he goes. His openness is the sole and sufficient justification for his ostracism. Though unintended, reliance on such a justification is tantamount to a constitutionally prescribed symbol of inferiority.

41. 430 U.S. 705 (1977).
42. *Id.* at 713.
43. *Id.* at 715.
44. *Id.* at 717.
45. *Id.* at 715.
46. James Madigan, *Questioning the Coercive Effect of Self-Identifying Speech,* 87 Iowa L. Rev. 75, 108 (2001).
47. *Id.* at 94. Accord *Dale,* 530 U.S. at 694 (Stevens, J., dissenting) ("[Dale's] participation sends no cognizable message to the Scouts or to the world.").
48. See *Clark v. Community for Creative Non-Violence,* 468 U.S. 288 (1984) (finding that sleeping while camping overnight on public land is not inherently expressive activity and can receive First Amendment protection, if at all, only under the *O'Brien* standard for expressive conduct).

49. For a useful short overview of the philosophical literature on semantic meaning, see Matthew D. Adler, *Expressive Theories of Law: A Skeptical Overview,* 148 U. Penn. L. Rev. 1363, 1384–96 (2000).

50. "All Things Considered" on National Public Radio, June 28, 2000, available in LEXIS, News Library, NPR file. Justice Scalia evidently took a different view during the oral argument:

> You think it does not limit the ability of the Boy Scouts to convey its message to require the Boy Scouts to have as a Scout master someone who embodies a contradiction of its message, whether the person wears a sign or not? But if the person is publicly known to be an embodiment of the — of a contradiction of its moral message, how can that not dilute the message?

Transcript of oral argument, *Boy Scouts of America v. Dale,* 2000 WL 489419, at 27–28.

51. See Steven D. Smith, *Symbols, Perceptions, and Doctrinal Illusions: Establishment Neutrality and the "No Endorsement" Test,* 86 Mich. L. Rev. 266 (1987).

52. See *id.* at 325–31.

53. Of course, some minorities may perceive a message where none is intended or perceived by the majority, and the minority's pertinent background assumptions are sometimes more attractive than the majority's.

54. Here is one illustration, from the French Revolution:

> The execution of the Hebertists implied that of the Dantonists also. If they were left alive after their opponents had been killed their position would be relatively stronger, and it would appear that the Committee had acted at their command. The unity of the Committee was also at stake, for Billaud-Varenne and Collot d'Herbois could not have been expected to accept the suppression of the extremists unless the moderates were also destroyed.

M. J. Sydenham, The French Revolution 212 (1965). Similar logic was used for many years to maintain the criminalization of homosexual sex: if the law stopped hunting down gays' private sex acts, it was successfully argued, this would implicitly send a message of approval. See William N.

Eskridge Jr., *No Promo Homo: The Sedimentation of Antigay Discourse and the Channeling Effect of Judicial Review,* 75 N.Y.U. L. Rev. 1327, 1339–46 (2000).

55. 163 U.S. 537 (1896).

56. *Id.* at 550.

57. See generally Charles S. Mangum Jr., The Legal Status of the Negro 18–25 (1940). The argument for so holding was succinctly stated by one court:

> Under the social habits, customs and prejudices prevailing in Louisiana, it cannot be disputed that charging a white man with being a Negro is calculated to inflict injury and damage. We are concerned with these social conditions simply as facts. They exist, and for that reason we deal with them. No one could make such a charge, knowing it to be false, without understanding that its effect would be injurious and without intending to injure.

Sportono v. Fourichon, 4 So. 71, 71 (La. 1888); quoted with approval in *Flood v. News and Courier Co.,* 50 S.E. 637, 639–40 (S.C. 1905). See also *Wolfe v. Georgia Ry. & Elec. Co.,* 58 S.E. 899, 902 (1907) ("neither legislatures nor courts shall grade the citizen according to his social status, and yet . . . the courts can and must know and notice the meaning of words of opprobrium as well as the connection in which these words are used."). Courts have now abandoned this doctrine but have not clearly explained the reasons for the abandonment. See Lyrissa Barnett Lidsky, *Defamation, Reputation, and the Myth of Community,* 71 Wash L. Rev. 1, 28–36 (1996) (discussing recent cases).

58. 466 U.S. 429 (1984) (holding that societal prejudice is not a valid reason for a court to disprefer an interracial couple in a child custody dispute).

59. *Id.* at 433.

60. Compare *Employment Division v. Smith,* 494 U.S. 872 (1990).

61. See, e.g., *Strauder v. West Virginia,* 100 U.S. 303, 308 (1880); *Brown v. Board of Educ.,* 347 U.S. 483, 494 (1954).

62. Thus, David Bernstein is too charitable to the Court when he writes that "the underlying moral rectitude of BSA's exclusion of homosexuals was not legally relevant in *Dale.*" Bernstein, *Antidiscrimination Laws,* at 88.

63. The car manufacturer is primarily a commercial rather an expressive

association, but again, businesses are protected against compelled speech. See *supra* note 34.

64. *United States v. O'Brien*, 391 U.S. 367, 377 (1968).

65. Daniel A. Farber, The First Amendment 26 (1998).

66. See *United States v. United Foods*, 533 U.S. 405, 413–14 (2001); *Abood v. Detroit Board of Educ.*, 431 U.S. 209, 222 (1977).

67. Robert Post, *Transparent and Efficient Markets: Compelled Commercial Speech and Coerced Commercial Association in* United Foods, Zauderer, *and* Abood, 40 Val. U. L. Rev. 555, 585 (2006).

68. *Roberts v. United States Jaycees*, 468 U.S. 609, 623 (1984).

69. 530 U.S. at 659.

70. 530 U.S. 567 (2000).

71. *Dale* was announced June 28, 2000; *Jones* was announced June 26.

72. *Jones,* 530 U.S. at 582.

73. Samuel Issacharoff, *Private Parties with Public Purposes: Political Parties, Associational Freedoms, and Partisan Competition,* 101 Colum. L. Rev. 274 (2001).

Chapter 3. The Solomon Amendment Litigation and Other Consequences of *Dale*

1. 547 U.S. 47 (2006).

2. *Forum for Academic and Institutional Rights (FAIR) v. Rumsfeld*, 390 F.3d 219 (3d Cir. 2004); rev'd, 547 U.S. 47 (2006).

3. *Burt v. Rumsfeld*, 354 F. Supp.2d 156 (D. Conn. 2005).

4. The facts that follow are drawn largely from the summary provided in *Burt v. Rumsfeld.*

5. See *FAIR,* 390 F.3d at 224–25 (recounting AALS's expansion of its non-discrimination policy).

6. The current policy, colloquially known as "Don't Ask, Don't Tell," was enacted by statute in 1993 and took effect in early 1994. See 10 U.S.C. 654, "Policy Concerning Homosexuality in the Military." The policy imposes unique and extraordinarily burdensome restrictions on speech and conduct upon gay, lesbian, and bisexual servicemembers, effectively forcing them to remain closeted and celibate, and to affect a straight identity, as the condition of military service. See generally Tobias Barrington Wolff, *Political Representation and Accountability under Don't Ask, Don't Tell,* 89

Iowa L. Rev. 1633 (2004) (describing operation of policy). Before Don't Ask, Don't Tell, the military maintained a blanket ban on service by gay, lesbian, and bisexual soldiers, a policy that it imposed through executive and administrative command rather than statutory mandate. In practice, Don't Ask, Don't Tell has operated in a manner that is similar in many ways to the blanket ban that preceded it. The rate at which gay servicemembers are discharged has been higher in some years under Don't Ask, Don't Tell, despite President Bill Clinton's promise at the time of its enactment that the new policy would create a space within which gay men and lesbians could serve. See generally Servicemembers Legal Defense Network, 10 Year Timeline of "Don't Ask, Don't Tell," available at http://www.sldn.org/templates/dadt/record.html?section=183&record=1449 (last visited Aug. 9, 2007).

7. This is not the place to take up the unresolved question of what actual effect the law school policies might have had upon the ability of the military to satisfy its recruitment goals in the various JAG Corps, but that threat is easily overstated. The common shorthand description that one often hears of the manner in which law schools sought to enforce their nondiscrimination policies — "The law schools were trying to exclude military recruiters" — can easily give the false impression that JAG was being prevented from interviewing law students altogether. The reality is far different. No law school ever forbade its students to interview with JAG, and most permitted JAG to participate in some fashion in the normal interview season. Generally, schools merely requested that JAG conduct its interviews off campus and contact interested students without the assistance of the law school placement office. See Brief for the Respondents, *Rumsfeld v. FAIR,* No. 04-1152 (Sept. 21, 2005) (hereinafter FAIR Main Brief), at 7–8 (setting forth undisputed account of accommodations requested by objecting law schools). Such policies imposed inconvenience on JAG recruiters, to be sure, and may have had some marginal effect on JAG's overall recruitment efforts. But the number of law students who interview with JAG recruiters is very small at most institutions; and law schools often do not offer a very affirming or friendly atmosphere for those interested in the military, for reasons having as much to do with class bias as with political views. This is particularly the case at rich and selective private institutions. As a consequence, those students who do wish to interview with JAG are usually a highly moti-

vated and self-directed group. While they may find it less pleasant and less convenient to interview under the conditions that the law schools sought to impose, law students who are interested in careers as military lawyers are likely to find their way to JAG even if they must overcome administrative inconvenience to do so.

8. The amendment currently provides as follows:

(b) Denial of funds for preventing military recruiting on campus. — No funds described in subsection (d)(1) may be provided by contract or by grant to an institution of higher education (including any subelement of such institution) if the Secretary of Defense determines that that institution (or any subelement of that institution) has a policy or practice (regardless of when implemented) that either prohibits, or in effect prevents —

(1) the Secretary of a military department or Secretary of Homeland Security from gaining access to campuses, or access to students (who are 17 years of age or older) on campuses, for purposes of military recruiting in a manner that is at least equal in quality and scope to the access to campuses and to students that is provided to any other employer; or

(2) access by military recruiters for purposes of military recruiting to the following information pertaining to students (who are 17 years of age or older) enrolled at that institution (or any subelement of that institution):

(A) Names, addresses, and telephone listings.

(B) Date and place of birth, levels of education, academic majors, degrees received, and the most recent educational institution enrolled in by the student.

10 U.S.C. 983(b).

9. See 61 Fed.Reg. 7739, 7740 (Feb. 29, 1996). Law schools do not typically receive a large amount of federal funding.

10. 10 U.S.C. 983(c)(2), as modified by Pub. L. No. 106-65, 549(a)(1) (1999); Defense Federal Acquisition Regulation Supplement: Institutions of Higher Education, 65 Fed.Reg. 2056 (Jan. 13, 2000). The effect of this redefinition was that a violation in any part of the university

would jeopardize federal funding for the entire university. 48 C.F.R. 252.209-7005.

11. The University of Pennsylvania Law School also brought a Solomon suit, which placed much greater emphasis on a claim that the institution was actually in compliance with the statutory mandate and asserted constitutional claims only in a subsidiary posture. That suit was partially dismissed at the district court level (for lack of standing and failure to state a cause of action on respective counts) and was then superseded by the decision of the Supreme Court before it produced any substantial constitutional ruling. See *Burbank v. Rumsfeld*, 2004 WL 1925532 (E.D. Pa., Aug. 26, 2004). Professor Wolff joined the faculty of the University of Pennsylvania Law School after the termination of this suit (and after the Supreme Court's decision in *FAIR*) and played no role in that litigation.

12. The ones described below are plausible ones, but here we note a few that are not. They are interesting primarily because the broad, vague *Dale* opinion evidently invites attorneys to reach for it whenever any kind of association is regulated. A high school football coach asserted the right to participate in student-initiated school prayer. The court held that expressive association rights do not extend to state employees while on duty. *Borden v. School Dist. of Tp. of East Brunswick*, 523 F.3d 153 (3d Cir. 2008). *Dale* challenges were also brought against a ban on smoking in public accommodations, *Taverns for Tots, Inc. v. City of Toledo*, 341 F.Supp.2d 844 (N.D. Ohio 2004); and against the criminal prosecution of an endless chain scheme, *Saunders v. Knight*, 2007 WL 3482047 (E.D. Cal. 2007).

13. When a motorcycle club whose members were not allowed to wear club insignia at a city-sponsored festival brought suit, the court found it necessary to deny that the insignia were expressive. *Villegas v. City of Gilroy*, 484 F.3d 1136, 1142 (9th Cir. 2007). In a challenge to a city ordinance prohibiting commercial sex clubs, the court relied on its finding that as a matter of law the sex in the clubs was not expressive conduct, implying that if that sex had been intended to send some kind of message, the claim would have been stronger. *Recreational Developments of Phoenix v. City of Phoenix*, 220 F.Supp.2d 1054, 1067 (D. Ariz. 2002). (Sex by exhibitionists might present a hard case.) Upholding a state university's decision to strip a fraternity of its status as a recognized student organization where it was found that members had abused illegal drugs, the court relied on the fact that the fraternity had never taken "a public stance on any issue of

public political, social, or cultural importance." *Pi Lambda Phi Fraternity v. Univ. of Pittsburgh*, 229 F.3d 435, 444 (2000). See also *Beta Upsilon Chi v. Machen*, 559 F.Supp.2d 1274, 1278 (N.D. Fla. 2008) (denying injunction against application of nondiscrimination policy to religious fraternity); *Chi Iota Colony of Alpha Epsilon Pi Fraternity v. City University of New York*, 502 F.3d 136 (2d Cir. 2007) (upholding right of state college to withhold recognition from all-male fraternity; reversing lower court that had relied on *Dale*).

14. A city tried, unsuccessfully, to invoke *Dale* to justify the expulsion of a speaker from a public park that was being used by a private permittee for an event open to the public, when the permittee deemed the speaker to be interfering with the permittee's message. *Dale*'s holding, the court reasoned, "was grounded in whether the plaintiff's views could be mistaken for those of the defendant." *Gathright v. City of Portland*, 439 F.3d 573, 578 (9th Cir. 2006). See also *Wickersham v. City of Columbia*, 2006 WL 4748740 (W.D. Mo. 2006), in which a city tried, unsuccessfully, to invoke *Dale* to justify the expulsion of demonstrators from an air show that was open to the public.

15. A gun control statute limiting the use of certain weapons to licensed gun clubs (effectively pressuring nonmembers to join such clubs) was upheld because the gun owners "are not being forced to join any association that espouses a political viewpoint, and are not required to permit persons whose viewpoints they find objectionable to join their own association." *Gun Owners' Action League, Inc. v. Swift*, 284 F.3d 198, 215–16 (1st Cir. 2002). The use of undercover officers to enforce a prohibition against "lap dancing" was upheld because the clubs were not required to accept the undercover police officers as members, but did so voluntarily (albeit ignorantly). *City of Shoreline v. Club for Free Speech Rights*, 36 P.3d 1058, 707–08 (2001). In yet another fraternity case, the court wrote: "The withdrawal of recognition did not in and of itself deprive Chapter members of their First Amendment rights. Nothing in the University's sanction prevents the Chapter from continuing to exist." *Iota XI Chapter of the Sigma Chi Fraternity v. Patterson*, 538 F.Supp.2d 915, 923 (E.D. Va. 2008).

16. *Central Texas Nudists v. County of Travis*, 2000 WL 1784344 (Tex. App. Austin 2000).

17. 808 N.Y.S.2d 447 (N.Y.A.D. 3d Dept. 2006).

18. *Id.* at 459.

19. *Id.* at 460.
20. *Id.* at 473 (Cardona, J., dissenting), quoting *Dale,* 530 U.S. at 656.
21. *Id.*
22. *Hyman v. City of Louisville,* 132 F.Supp.2d 528, 544 (W.D. Ky. 2001), quoting *Hishon v. King & Spalding,* 467 U.S. 69, 78 (1984), which in turn was quoting *Norwood v. Harrison,* 413 U.S. 455, 470 (1973). After *Dale,* of course, this sentence can no longer be accepted without modification, but the *Hyman* court ignored this complexity.
23. *Lahmann v. Grand Aerie of Fraternal Order of Eagles,* 121 P.3d 671, 685 (Or. App. 2005). See also *Fraternal Order of Eagles, Tenino Aerie No. 564 v. Grand Aerie of Fraternal Order of Eagles,* 148 Wash.2d 224, 59 P.3d 655 (Wash. 2002) (similar result, with majority opinion ignoring *Dale* over the protest of dissenting judge).
24. A fourth was reversed on appeal to the Supreme Court. See *Washington State Public Disclosure Comm'n v. Washington Education Ass'n,* 130 P.2d 352 (Wash. 2006), rev'd sub. nom. *Davenport v. Washington Education Assn.,* 127 S.Ct. 2372 (2007). The Court followed the *Rumsfeld v. FAIR* decision, discussed below, by holding that a statute does not violate freedom of association if it "does not compel [an association's] acceptance of unwanted members or otherwise make . . . membership less attractive." 127 S.Ct. at 2380 n.2. Another case that might appear relevant is *Circle Schools v. Pappert,* 381 F.3d 172 (3d Cir. 2004), holding that a statute, in requiring private schools to provide for recitation of the Pledge of Allegiance or national anthem at the beginning of each school day, violated private schools' First Amendment right to freedom of expressive association. The court cited *Dale,* but the same result could have been reached under much older compelled-speech precedents; the innovations of *Dale* were not necessary to the result.
25. *Chicago Council of Boy Scouts of America v. City of Chicago,* 748 N.E.2d 759 (Ill. 1st Dist. 2001), appeal denied, 763 N.E.2d 316 (Ill. 2001); *Boy Scouts of Am. v. D.C. Comm. on Human Rights,* 809 A.2d 1192 (D.C. 2002); see also *Boy Scouts of America, South Florida Council v. Till,* 136 F.Supp.2d 1295 (S.D. Fla. 2001) (public school is a limited public forum that cannot exclude the BSA from meeting space because of disagreement with viewpoint). But even the Scouts have gotten only limited mileage from *Dale.* The city of Berkeley was not prevented from revoking the BSA's privilege of docking its boats rent-free in the city's marina. See *Evans v. City of*

Berkeley, 129 P.2d 394 (Cal.), cert. denied, 127 S.Ct. 434 (2006). Nor was the state of Connecticut barred from excluding the BSA from its state employees' charitable campaign. *Boy Scouts of America v. Wyman*, 335 F.3d 80 (2d Cir. 2003), cert. denied, 541 U.S. 903 (2004). See also *Barnes-Wallace v. City of San Diego*, 471 F.3d 1038 (9th Cir. 2006) (avoiding federal question by certifying to California Supreme Court question of whether leasing of public parkland to the BSA violated religion clauses of state constitution).

26. *Donaldson v. Farrakhan*, 762 N.E.2d 835 (Mass. 2002). The internal autonomy of religious groups is a well-established doctrine that has been held to survive the holding of *Employment Division v. Smith*, 494 U.S. 872 (1990), that (as a general matter) the free exercise clause does not authorize the courts to carve out exemptions to generally applicable laws when such laws burden religious activities. See *Combs v. Central Texas Annual Conference of the United Methodist Church*, 173 F.3d 343 (5th Cir. 1999); *E.E.O.C. v. Catholic University of America*, 83 F.3d 455 (D.C. Cir. 1996). The general weakness of *Dale* claims in nonreligious contexts has implications for the theory of religious liberty. It shows why one cannot rely on *Dale* to explain the fact that, for example, the Catholic Church is allowed to discriminate on the basis of sex in selecting priests. Christopher L. Eisgruber and Lawrence G. Sager depend on this dubious reading of *Dale* to support their claim that this discrimination would still be permitted in their proposed regime, in which religious as such would get no special benefits. Religious Freedom and the Constitution 64–65 (2007). On the limitations of Eisgruber and Sager's account of religious liberty, see Andrew Koppelman, *Is It Fair to Give Religion Special Treatment?*, 2006 U. of Ill. L. Rev. 571.

27. In recent years, federal courts have been considering several challenges brought by Christian student organizations seeking exemptions from their institutions' antidiscrimination policies. In one such challenge, decided after the Supreme Court's decision in *FAIR*, the Seventh Circuit provided the organization with the exemption that it sought. See *Christian Legal Soc'y v. Walker*, 453 F.3d 853 (7th Cir. 2006). The court in this case appears to have employed a much more robust form of factual analysis than would be called for under the "*Dale* deference" doctrine. In addition, the court concluded that the defendant sought to apply its policy to the student group because of its disapproval of the group's

viewpoint — an assertion that, if true, would bring the holding of the case squarely within the ambit of *Roberts* (discussed in Chapter 1), with no need even to advert to the more expansive features of *Dale*. See *Roberts v. U.S. Jaycees*, 468 U.S. 609, 623–24 (1984).

28. See the U.S. Junior Chamber Jaycees, http://www.usjaycees.org/learn_more.htm (last visited July 4, 2007).

29. *Roberts*, 468 U.S. at 625–26.

30. *Id.* at 629–30.

31. The law professors emphasized this distinction and explicitly invited the Court to extend *Dale* beyond the context of membership interference. See, e.g., FAIR Main Brief, *supra* note 7, at 17 ("The freedom of association is not limited to circumstances in which the government interferes with an organization's internal composition, but extends to the full range of causes an expressive organization may choose to embrace or reject."). See also *id.* at 31–32 (elaborating on this argument).

32. Don't Ask, Don't Tell itself does not deal directly with gender identity or the treatment of transgendered individuals, though the military treats trans people with swift and reliable hostility through other policies.

33. FAIR Main Brief, *supra* note 7, at 14. See also *id.*: "Faculty attest to student expressions of cynicism and cries of hypocrisy when the lessons turn to topics such as equality, human dignity, and other underpinnings of a just society. They feel inhibited to preach about integrity, adhering to principle, and fighting for a worthy cause" (citations omitted). "Preach" is not a felicitous term for the pedagogical responsibility of a law professor. The *FAIR* litigation was predicated on a vision of the university in which faculty are unable to communicate their ideas effectively unless they are able to exclude those who propound ideas inconsistent with their own. That vision betrays the institutional function of the university. This objection is beyond the scope of this book; it is elaborated in Tobias Barrington Wolff and Andrew Koppelman, *Expressive Association and the Ideal of the University in the Solomon Amendment Litigation*, 25 Soc. Phil. & Pol'y 92, 118–22 (2008).

34. Under *Dale*, it was arguably the case that the law professors were required only to show that the inclusion of the military recruiters "significantly affect[ed]" their ability to propound their message, even if it did not undermine the message altogether. This is the standard that the Third Circuit purported to apply, see *FAIR v. Rumsfeld*, 390 F.3d 219, 231–34

(3d Cir. 2003), and FAIR adopted the Third Circuit's analysis wholesale in its briefs. See FAIR Main Brief, *supra* note 7, at 30. However, any such distinctions are rendered irrelevant by the Third Circuit's further conclusion that it was required to apply *"Dale* deference" to any claim that FAIR made of interference with its expression, whatever the magnitude of that claimed interference. See *FAIR,* 390 F.3d at 233–34. As Justice Souter once wrote in a different context, "The sequence of the Court's positions prompts a suspicion of error, and skepticism is confirmed by scrutiny of the Court's efforts to justify its holding." *Alden v. Maine,* 527 U.S. 706, 761 (1999) (Souter, J., dissenting). Had the Supreme Court accepted the invitation to place substantial weight on the lesser "significantly affects" standard, the more permissive standard might have made the plaintiffs' claims somewhat more plausible on the facts (though not much). It would also, however, have resulted in a change in the law — the application of even more expansive *"Dale* deference" to every entity that engages in any form of expression.

35. Title IX, like the Solomon Amendment, operates as a condition upon the receipt of federal funds, and any institution seeking to pursue such a claim might have to grapple with the particular set of requirements associated with spending clause doctrine. But the very fact that Title IX would be subject to the threat of a robust First Amendment defense in such cases would constitute a dramatic change. In *Grove City College v. Bell,* 465 U.S. 555 (1984), in contrast, the Court avoided any First Amendment analysis by concluding that individual recipients of federal funds were free to decline them, presenting no threat to First Amendment values. The entirety of the Court's analysis is contained in the following passage:

> Grove City's final challenge to the Court of Appeals' decision — that conditioning federal assistance on compliance with Title IX infringes First Amendment rights of the College and its students — warrants only brief consideration. Congress is free to attach reasonable and unambiguous conditions to federal financial assistance that educational institutions are not obligated to accept. Grove City may terminate its participation in the BEOG program and thus avoid the requirements of 901(a). Students affected by the Department's action may either take their BEOGs elsewhere or attend Grove City without federal financial assistance. Requiring

> Grove City to comply with Title IX's prohibition of discrimination as a condition for its continued eligibility to participate in the BEOG program infringes no First Amendment rights of the College or its students.

Id. at 575–76. This dismissive holding clearly could not survive a robust application of *Dale,* and it has questionable continuing vitality in any event because of the passage by Congress of the Civil Rights Restoration Act of 1987, 20 U.S.C. 1987, which overruled *Grove City*'s interpretation of Title IX and threatened the withdrawal of federal funds from entire educational institutions when any component or program of the institution engages in discrimination, resulting in significantly greater coercive pressure.

36. As noted in Chapter 1, the Supreme Court dismissed an argument along these lines out of hand in *Runyon v. McCrary.* As noted in Chapter 2, the *Dale* Court denied that it was offering a blanket exemption from antidiscrimination law for any entity that wanted to claim a right to associate. *Runyon* was decided at a time when the Court's expressive association doctrine was still at an early stage of development, and the brevity of its treatment of the issue in an opinion that was primarily focused on other matters has meant that *Runyon*'s effect in this arena has been limited. Nonetheless, it is difficult to imagine the Court overruling the result in that case. Members of the Harvard Law School faculty raised a similar set of concerns about the effect of FAIR's arguments on antidiscrimination laws in an amicus curiae brief, urging the Supreme Court to confine its ruling to statutory rather than constitutional grounds. See *Rumsfeld v FAIR*, Brief of Professors William Alford et al., 2006 WL 2367595.

37. FAIR's response to this threat was to argue that, as a matter of constitutional policy, antidiscrimination laws should continue to prevail even in the face of robust *Dale*-style First Amendment arguments because discrimination suffers from particular disfavor under the Constitution. See FAIR Main Brief, *supra* note 7, at 34–35. Of course, this argument did not prevail in the *Dale* case itself.

38. Rumsfeld v. FAIR, 547 U.S. 47, 60 (2006).

39. *Id.* at 69, quoting *Dale,* 530 U.S. at 648 (which in turn was quoting *Roberts,* 468 U.S. at 623).

40. *Id.* at 60–65.

41. This unsatisfying explanation leaves in place *Dale*'s nasty suggestion that the inclusion of a gay member is inherently expressive (and hence raises First Amendment problems that are particular to gay people), but at least the Court's opinion did not give any further credence to this idea.

42. For a similar gesture of limitation, see *Davenport v. Washington Education Assn.*, 127 S.Ct. 2372, 2380 n.2 (2007) (indicating that a law does not violate *Dale* if it "does not compel . . . acceptance of unwanted members or otherwise make . . . membership less attractive").

43. 128 S.Ct. 1184 (2008).

44. *Id.* at 1193.

45. *Id.* at 1194.

46. *Id.*

47. *Id.* at 1194 n.9.

48. *Id.* at 1197 (Roberts, C.J., concurring).

49. *Id.* at 1196.

50. *Id.* at 1198 (Scalia, J., dissenting).

51. *Id.* at 1200.

52. *Id.* at 1201.

53. *Id.*

54. Justice Scalia made the analogy explicit. See *id.* at 1203 ("Washington's electoral system permits individuals to appropriate the parties' trademarks, so to speak, at the most crucial stage of election, thereby distorting the parties' messages and impairing their endorsement of candidates.").

Chapter 4. The Neolibertarian Proposal

1. Dale Carpenter, *Expressive Association and Anti-Discrimination Law after Dale: A Tripartite Approach,* 85 Minn. L. Rev. 1515, 1517 (2001).

2. Michael Stokes Paulsen, *Scouts, Families, and Schools,* 85 Minn. L. Rev. 1917, 1922 (2001). For this he cites Akhil Amar's historical work on the speech and assembly clauses, but Amar's scholarship does not help him. The right of the people to assemble, Amar observes, "referred to formal gatherings of voters—who else could presume to instruct lawmakers?—rather than mere informal clumps of self-selected persons seeking to associate." Akhil Reed Amar, The Bill of Rights: Creation and Reconstruction 29 (1998). It has no obvious implications for the freedom of nonpolitical groups to discriminate.

3. Paulsen, *Scouts, Families, and Schools,* at 1922.

4. For similar arguments, see Carpenter, *Expressive Association and Anti-Discrimination Law,* at 1535–36 n.99; Seana Valentine Shiffrin, *What Is Really Wrong with Compelled Association?,* 99 Nw. U. L. Rev. 839, 864–73 (2005).

5. Elsewhere Paulsen acknowledges that "[f]ew these days would take seriously an employer's argument that racially discriminatory employment practices are protected as 'free speech.'" Michael Paulsen, *A Funny Thing Happened on the Way to the Limited Public Forum: Unconstitutional Conditions on "Equal Access" for Religious Speakers and Groups,* 29 U.C. Davis L. Rev. 653, 676 (1996).

6. See Richard McAdams, *Cooperation and Conflict: The Economics of Group Status Production and Race Discrimination,* 108 Harv. L. Rev. 1003, 1074–82 (1995).

7. Robert Post, Prejudicial Appearances: The Logic of American Anti-discrimination Law (2001); Andrew Koppelman, Antidiscrimination Law and Social Equality (1996).

8. Paulsen, *Scouts, Families, and Schools,* at 1924.

9. *Id.* at 1927 n.49.

10. *Id.*

11. The potentially anarchic implication of a very broad reading of the First Amendment was noted long ago by Robert Bork. See Robert Bork, *Neutral Principles and Some First Amendment Problems,* 47 Ind. L.J. 1, 25–27 (1971). I am not entirely confident of my interpretation of Paulsen because in a few footnotes, he nearly takes it all back by suggesting that the appropriate test for a restriction on associational freedom is that of *United States v. O'Brien,* 391 U.S. 367 (1968) — a test that in practice has been even easier for the state to satisfy than the *Roberts* test. See, e.g., *City of Erie v. Pap's A.M.,* 529 U.S. 277 (2000). See Paulsen, *A Funny Thing,* at 692–93 n.93; Paulsen, *Scouts, Families, and Schools,* at 1936 n.86. (On the *Dale* Court's unpersuasive efforts to distinguish *O'Brien,* see Stephen Clark, *Judicially Straight? Boy Scouts v. Dale and the Missing Scalia Dissent,* 76 S. Cal. L. Rev. 521, 571–73 [2003].) If this is Paulsen's view, then he should not be classed as one of the neolibertarians, but then it would be hard to understand how he can support the result in *Dale,* as he obviously does.

12. See Richard Epstein, *The Constitutional Perils of Moderation: The Case of the Boy Scouts,* 74 S. Cal. L. Rev. 119, 139–40 (2000). Epstein concedes,

however, that it would be "bold and foolhardy" to claim that current law goes so far. *Id.* at 139.

13. See Carpenter, *Expressive Association and Anti-Discrimination Law,* at 1542–63.

14. Shiffrin, *What Is Really Wrong with Compelled Association?,* at 846.

15. *Id.* at 851.

16. Carpenter does devote a long discussion to the history of state-sponsored suppression of expressive associations, Carpenter, *Expressive Association and Anti-Discrimination Law,* at 1520–33, but all of the history he describes involves naked viewpoint discrimination and so would be unconstitutional even without any special doctrine protecting associational rights. Carpenter responds by noting the courts' ham-handed treatment of the groups' messages in *Roberts* and (in the lower courts) *Dale.* "Even if there aren't many examples yet I'm not sure this response is fair given that application of antidiscrimination laws to private, expressive organizations is itself a very recent development (perhaps the last two decades). Give it time, I predict, and the abuses would multiply." Personal communication, Oct. 19, 2003. He is right about *Roberts,* as I argue at the conclusion of Chapter 1. But there is no such trend. Most antidiscrimination laws have not been construed to apply to private nonexpressive organizations. See Jay M. Zitter, Annotation, *What constitutes private club or association not otherwise open to public that is exempt from state civil rights statute,* 83 A.L.R.5th 467 (2000). Even the New Jersey case is an outlier and might have been overruled by the legislature had the Court not intervened. Moreover, as I argue in Chapter 6, it is far from clear that New Jersey was wrong to apply its antidiscrimination law to the BSA.

17. "Imagine, for example, putting the fate of a gay organization's internal organizational rules in the hands of an elected judge in a state with an anti-gay sodomy law." Carpenter, *Expressive Association and Anti-Discrimination Law,* at 1549. The prospect is scary, but it is noteworthy that it hasn't happened yet. There is a history of pervasive viewpoint-based discrimination against gays, see Andrew Koppelman, *Why Gay Legal History Matters,* 113 Harv. L. Rev. 2035 (2000), but it considerably antedates *Roberts.*

18. Carpenter, *Expressive Association and Anti-Discrimination Law,* at 1587.

19. *Id.* at 1585–86.

20. Shiffrin, *What Is Really Wrong with Compelled Association?,* at 877.

21. Epstein, *Constitutional Perils,* at 128.

22. *Id.* at 129.

23. *Id.* at 131. For similar arguments, see Carpenter, *Expressive Association and Anti-Discrimination Law,* at 1547; Reply Brief for Petitioner, *Boy Scouts of America v. Dale,* 2000 WL 432367, at 4.

24. *Dale,* 530 U.S. at 656.

25. Brief for Petitioner, *Boy Scouts of America v. Dale,* 2000 WL 228616.

26. Michael W. McConnell, *The New Establishmentarianism,* 75 Chi.-Kent L. Rev. 453, 466 (2000).

27. Michael W. McConnell and Richard A. Posner, *An Economic Approach to Issues of Religious Freedom,* 56 U. Chi. L. Rev. 1, 60 (1989).

28. *Id.* at 14.

29. *Id.* at 11.

30. *Id.* at 47.

31. Michael W. McConnell, *Religious Freedom at a Crossroads,* 59 U. Chi. L. Rev. 115, 194 (1992).

32. *Id.* at 169.

33. This argument was previously made more briefly in Andrew Koppelman, *Secular Purpose,* 88 Va. L. Rev. 87, 152 (2002), and is defended against objections in Andrew Koppelman, *No Expressly Religious Orthodoxy: A Response to Steven D. Smith,* 78 Chi.-Kent L. Rev. 729 (2003).

34. See McConnell and Posner, *An Economic Approach,* at 6–7.

35. *Id.* at 33.

36. *Id.* at 46–51.

37. See Koppelman, *Secular Purpose,* at 110.

38. James Madison, *Memorial and Remonstrance against Religious Assessments,* in The Mind of the Founder: Sources of the Political Thought of James Madison 6 (Marvin Meyers, ed., rev. ed. 1981).

39. Nancy Rosenblum, Membership and Morals: The Personal Uses of Pluralism in America (1998).

40. *Id.* at 170.

41. John McGinnis, *Reviving Tocqueville's America: The Rehnquist Court's Jurisprudence of Social Discovery,* 90 Calif. L. Rev. 485, 489 (2002). For a critique of McGinnis's defense of the Rehnquist Court's work, see Andrew Koppelman, *How "Decentralization" Rationalizes Oligarchy: John McGinnis and the Rehnquist Court,* 20 Const. Comm. 11 (2003).

42. McGinnis, *Reviving Tocqueville's America,* at 533.

43. *Id.* at 534.
44. *Id.* at 535.
45. *Id.* at 538 n.268.
46. A similar defense of a broad freedom of association is offered in David E. Bernstein, You Can't Say That! The Growing Threat to Civil Liberties from Antidiscrimination Laws 97–110 (2003). Bernstein relies on McGinnis's claims, see *id.* at 103, but is even vaguer than McGinnis about the precise scope of the freedom of association that he wants to defend.
47. See Ronald J. Allen, *Constitutional Adjudication, the Demands of Knowledge, and Epistemological Modesty,* 88 Nw. U. L. Rev. 436 (1993).
48. 494 U.S. 872 (1990).
49. See Christopher L. Eisgruber and Lawrence G. Sager, *The Vulnerability of Conscience: The Constitutional Basis for Protecting Religious Conduct,* 61 U. Chi. L. Rev. 1245, 1277–82 (1994).
50. *Smith,* 321 U.S. at 886–87.
51. See *Church of the Lukumi Babalu Aye v. City of Hialeah,* 508 U.S. 520 (1993).
52. The anomaly of Scalia's providing the fifth vote in *Dale* is explored in detail in Clark, *Judicially Straight?* Carpenter devotes a long discussion to the history of state-sponsored suppression of expressive associations, Carpenter, *Expressive Association and Anti-Discrimination Law,* at 1520–33, but almost all of the history he describes involves naked viewpoint discrimination and so would violate the First Amendment even without any special doctrine protecting associational rights.
53. This is noted by Carpenter, *Expressive Association and Anti-Discrimination Law,* at 1539.
54. See *Jones v. Wolf,* 443 U.S. 595 (1979); *Serbian Eastern Orthodox Diocese v. Milivojevich,* 426 U.S. 696 (1976); *Presbyterian Church v. Hull Church,* 393 U.S. 440 (1969); *Watson v. Jones,* 80 U.S. 679 (1872).
55. See Koppelman, *Secular Purpose,* at 108–113.
56. This requirement is relevant to the autonomy of religious associations, which is why the *Dale* rule has been successfully invoked only by the BSA itself and religious groups such as the Nation of Islam. See Chapter 3, note 26. The exemption of religious groups from antidiscrimination law is in this way not an exception to *Smith* but an application of its principles.
57. Epstein, *Constitutional Perils,* at 130.
58. See Jennifer Gerarda Brown, *Facilitating Boycotts of Discriminatory Orga-*

nizations through an Informed Association Statute, 87 Minn. L. Rev. 481 (2002).

59. See Marc R. Poirier, *Hastening the* Kulturkampf: Boy Scouts of America v. Dale *and the Politics of American Masculinity,* 12 L. & Sexuality 271 (2003).

60. See *Diaz v. Pan American World Airways, Inc.,* 442 F.2d 385 (5th Cir. 1971).

61. Kimberly Yuracko, *Private Nurses and Playboy Bunnies: Explaining Permissible Sex Discrimination,* 92 Calif. L. Rev. 147, 196 (2004).

62. *Id.* at 205.

63. *Id.* at 205–06.

64. Carpenter, *Expressive Association and Anti-Discrimination Law,* at 1542.

65. *Id.* at 1556–57, footnotes omitted.

66. William P. Marshall, *Discrimination and the Right of Association,* 81 Nw. U. L. Rev. 68, 79 (1986).

67. 319 U.S. 624 (1943).

68. 468 U.S. 288 (1984).

69. George Sher, Beyond Neutrality: Perfectionism and Politics 73 (1997).

Chapter 5. Is the BSA Being as Bad as Racists?

1. The 2000 Annual Report of the Boy Scouts of America reported a total traditional membership of 3,351,969 (online at http://www.scouting .org). That number reported in the 2007 Annual Report was 2,855,833, a decrease of 14.8 percent. Except for one year (2001–2002), when membership rose by just over one thousand members, total membership has fallen each year since the *Dale* decision (as of December 2007; figures from published BSA annual reports).

2. For a list of companies that have withdrawn funding, see http://www .scoutingforall.org (visited Apr. 25, 2008).

3. See the Boy Scouts of America Equal Access Act of 2002, Pub. L. 107-110, 115 Stat. 1981, 20 U.S.C.A. 7905.

4. Voluminous anecdotal evidence of defections from the BSA may be found in recent issues of Lesbian/Gay Law Notes, available at http://www.qrd .org/www/usa/legal/lgln/ (visited May 9, 2008).

5. 2006 Report of the Treasurer, Boy Scouts of America, available at http:// dev2.scouting.org/990/2006tr.pdf (visited May 9, 2008).

6. Brief for Respondent, *Boy Scouts of America v. Dale,* 530 U.S. 640 (2000), 2000 WL 340276, at 1.

7. Thus, for example, the Scouting for All Alliance for Human Rights, an organization that seeks to induce the BSA to change its policy, writes on its Web page: "would we as a society tolerate the BSA discriminating against people of color? What if the Boy Scouts of America said, African American youth and adults were not allowed in Scouting? How would the American people respond?" See http://www.scoutingforall.org/al liance.shtml (visited Nov. 14, 2002). "Those in Scouting have an ethical and moral obligation to stand against the bigotry of its current leader-ship." See http://www.scoutingforall.org/aaic/positionnc.shtml (vis-ited Nov. 14, 2002).

8. See Andrew Koppelman, The Gay Rights Question in Contemporary American Law 72–93 (2002); Andrew Koppelman, *Is Marriage Inher-ently Heterosexual?*, 42 Am. J. Jurisprudence 51 (1997).

9. The number of Americans who think that "homosexuality should be considered an acceptable alternative lifestyle" has been steadily rising, from 34 percent in 1982 to 57 percent in 2007. See Gallup Organization, Lydia Saad, Tolerance for Gay Rights at High-Water Mark: Public evenly divided over whether homosexuality is morally acceptable or wrong (May 29, 2007), available at http://institution.gallup.com/content/default.asp x?ci=27694&pg=1 (visited May 9, 2008).

10. Boy Scouts of America, Traditional Values and Standards (provided to "60 Minutes"), http://www.scouting.org/excomm/60minutes/60minu tes.html (visited May 15, 2002). (As of May 9, 2008, this document had disappeared from the BSA's Web page.)

11. *Id.*

12. Indeed, the authors of this book have different views on the matter. This chapter reflects the outlook of the book's principal author, Professor Kop-pelman. Professor Wolff is less convinced of the utility of entertaining a distinction between status and conduct as a means of framing arguments about equality. But, perhaps reflecting the inevitable complexity of work-ing through these issues in a legal world that has not yet fully internalized principles of lesbian, gay, bisexual, and transsexual equality, Professor Wolff has used a similar device in analyzing the proper treatment of same-sex relationships in interjurisdictional disputes. See Tobias Barrington Wolff, *Interest Analysis in Interjurisdictional Marriage Disputes,* 153 U. Penn. L. Rev. 2215, 2237 (2005) ("If one starts from the presumption that a state may forbid gay couples from marrying in the first place —

which I do, for purposes of this Article — then there will sometimes be legitimate interests that a state might invoke in refusing to give effect to a marriage performed in another state.").

13. Another objection is that the distinction between status and conduct, though theoretically coherent, is not consistently relied upon by those who seek to police "homosexual conduct," and that these policings in application disrupt the distinction that I have been relying on here. Thus, for example, Janet Halley has shown that the military's prohibition of "homosexual conduct" goes far beyond specified sex acts; it now makes members vulnerable to discharge for "[d]oing things that make your commander think you are gay — like making pro-gay statements, or cutting your hair a certain way, or not fitting the gender stereotype of the sex you belong to." Janet E. Halley, Don't: A Reader's Guide to the Military's Anti-Gay Policy 2 (1999). Evidently, what makes conduct homosexual is that it is a homosexual who is engaging in the conduct. See *id.*; Janet E. Halley, *The Politics of the Closet: Towards Equal Protection for Gay, Lesbian, and Bisexual Identity,* 36 U.C.L.A. L. Rev. 915 (1989); Janet E. Halley, *Misreading Sodomy: A Critique of the Classification of "Homosexuals" in Federal Equal Protection Law,* in Body Guards: The Cultural Politics of Gender Ambiguity 351 (Julia Epstein and Kristina Straub eds., 1991). These difficulties are not, however, necessarily present in all discriminations against people who engage in homosexual conduct. Halley's critique is devastating precisely because it exposes the status-based character of discrimination that is usually defended as conduct-based. Halley's investigations thus show the military's policy, and many other antigay policies, to be both hypocritical and vulnerable to the kind of syllogism with which this chapter begins. But this kind of sophisticated analysis is unnecessary with respect to the BSA's policy, which is overtly and unapologetically status-based.

14. See George Sher, Desert (1987), esp. pp. 37–40.

15. For a similar argument grounded in American constitutional law, see Andrew Koppelman, Antidiscrimination Law and Social Equality 65 (1996).

16. Kwame Anthony Appiah, In My Father's House: Africa in the Philosophy of Culture 14 (1992).

17. *Id.* at 15.

18. Mary Douglas, Purity and Danger: An Analysis of the Concepts of Pollution and Taboo 2 (1966).

19. *Id.*

20. *Id.* at 36.

21. *Id.* at 42.

22. *Id.* at 40.

23. *Id.* at 61–62.

24. *Dred Scott v. Sandford*, 60 U.S. (19 How.) 393, 407 (1857).

25. Charles L. Black Jr., *The Lawfulness of the Segregation Decisions*, 69 Yale L.J. 421, 426 (1960).

26. Richard A. Wasserstrom, *Racism, Sexism, and Preferential Treatment: An Approach to the Topics*, 24 U.C.L.A. L. Rev. 581, 592 (1977).

27. See Andrew Koppelman, Antidiscrimination Law and Social Equality 92–99 (1996).

28. Racial attitudes have been transformed dramatically in the past half-century. "At least until the 1940s, segregation, discrimination, and openly verbalized prejudice toward minorities of all kinds were entirely acceptable throughout much of the United States." Howard Schuman et al., Racial Attitudes in America: Trends and Interpretations 3 (rev. ed. 1997). Today, nearly all white Americans endorse principles of equal treatment. *Id.* at 103–21. For example, only 32 percent of white respondents endorsed racially integrated schools in 1942, whereas 96 percent did in 1995. *Id.* at 104–05.

29. A 1996 Washington Post poll found that 53 percent of respondents nationwide thought that racism is "a big problem" in our society, and 35 percent thought it was "somewhat of a problem." Eugene Robinson, *Black and White Getting By,* Wash. Post, July 15, 1996, at A1.

30. "[I]t is possible to bring societal pressure, indeed public shame, on any white American who clearly discriminates against blacks, provided that the discrimination can be brought to light, as in videotapes of police beatings, audiotapes of corporate obstruction of equal opportunity laws, or public remarks that impugn African Americans. The application of the term 'racist' to a person or organization is itself a severe sanction in most parts of the country." Schuman et al., Racial Attitudes in America, at 326–27.

31. Of course, effects are evidence of intentions, and vice versa; and social meaning is evidence of both. See Shari Seidman Diamond and Andrew Koppelman, *Measured Endorsement,* 60 Md. L. Rev. 713, 732 (2001); Andrew Koppelman, *On the Moral Foundations of Legal Expressivism,* 60 Md. L. Rev. 777 (2001).

32. *Bob Jones University v. United States*, 461 U.S. 574, 580 (1984), footnote omitted.

33. See Andrew Koppelman, *Why Discrimination against Lesbians and Gay Men Is Sex Discrimination*, 69 N.Y.U. L. Rev. 197, 220–34 (1994).

34. *Dred Scott v. Sandford*, 60 U.S. (19 How.) 393, 409 (1857).

35. Hendrik Hertzberg, *Comment: Bad News for Bigots*, New Yorker, Mar. 13, 2000, at 29–30.

36. When the university's leader, Bob Jones III, announced the change, he acknowledged the role of public opinion in the decision: "This thing is of such insignificance to us; it is so significant to the world at large, the media particularly, why should we have this here as an obstacle? It hurts our graduates . . . It hurts maybe the church as well. I don't want to hurt the church of Jesus Christ." Editorial, *Bob Jones Rules*, Christianity Today, Apr. 24, 2000, p. 41.

37. Richard Isay, Being Homosexual: Gay Men and Their Development 11 (1989). Isay is referring only to gay men, but his definition is transferable to lesbians, and I have so modified it.

38. In a survey of antigay violence and harassment in eight major cities,

> 86.2% of the gay men and women surveyed stated that they had been attacked verbally; 44.2% reported that they had been threatened with violence; 27.3% had had objects thrown at them; 34.9% had been chased or followed; 13.9% had been spit at; 19.2% had been punched, hit, kicked, or beaten; 9.3% had been assaulted with a weapon; 18.5% had been the victims of property vandalism or arson; 30.9% reported sexual harassment, many by members of their own families or by the police.

National Gay Task Force, Anti-Gay/Lesbian Victimization 24 (June 1984). These results have been replicated in other studies. See Kevin T. Berrill, *Anti-Gay Violence and Victimization in the United States: An Overview*, in Hate Crimes: Confronting Violence against Lesbians and Gay Men 19–45 (Gregory M. Herek and Kevin Berrill, eds., 1992); Gary David Comstock, Violence against Lesbians and Gay Men (1991). A study commissioned by the National Institute of Justice, the research arm of the U.S. Department of Justice, found that gays "are probably the most frequent victims [of hate violence today]." Peter Finn and Taylor McNeil,

The Response of the Criminal Justice System to Bias Crime: An Exploratory Review 2 (1987).

39. See Andrew Koppelman, Romer v. Evans *and Invidious Intent,* 6 Wm. & Mary Bill of Rts. J. 89, 125 (1997) (quoting Gordon W. Allport, The Nature of Prejudice 14, 49, 57, 59 [1954]).

40. Kenneth Sherrill, *The Political Power of Lesbians, Gays, and Bisexuals,* PS 469, 470 (1996).

41. *Id.*

42. Morris P. Fiorina et al., Culture War? The Myth of Polarized America 112 (2d ed. 2006).

43. See Jerry Kang, *Trojan Horses of Race,* 118 Harv. L. Rev. 1489 (2005); Tali Mendelberg, The Race Card: Campaign Strategy, Implicit Messages, and the Norm of Equality (2001).

44. Richard Mohr, A More Perfect Union: Why Straight America Must Stand Up for Gay Rights 61–62 (1994).

45. Quoted in Jules Witcover, Marathon: The Pursuit of the Presidency, 1972–1976 at 603 (1978).

46. John D'Emilio and Estelle B. Freedman, Intimate Matters: A History of Sexuality in America 293 (1988); John D'Emilio, The Homosexual Menace: The Politics of Sexuality in Cold War America, in Making Trouble: Essays on Gay History, Politics, and the University 57–73 (1992). The most thorough study to date of the legal status of gays during the antigay hysteria that prevailed in the decade and a half after World War II is William N. Eskridge Jr., Gaylaw: Challenging the Apartheid of the Closet (1999).

47. Committee on Expenditures in Executive Departments, Employment of Homosexuals and Other Sex Perverts in Government, U.S. Senate, 81st Cong., 2nd Sess., S. Doc. 81-241, at 4 (1950).

48. American Association of University Women, Hostile Hallways: The AAUW Survey on Sexual Harassment in America's Schools 20, 23 (1993). See also Deborah Brake, *The Cruelest of the Gender Police: Student-to-Student Sexual Harassment and Anti-Gay Peer Harassment under Title IX,* 1 Geo. J. Gender & L. 37 (1999).

49. William Marsiglio, *Attitudes toward Homosexual Activity and Gays as Friends: A National Survey of Heterosexual 15- to 19-Year-Old Males,* 30 J. Sex Res. 12 (1993).

50. See Safe Schools Coalition of Washington State, They Don't Even Know

Me: Understanding Anti-Gay Harassment and Violence in the Schools (1999). See also Gay, Lesbian, and Straight Educational Network, the 2005 National School Climate Survey, http://www.glsen.org/cgi-bin/ iowa/all/library/record/1927.html (visited May 9, 2008); Human Rights Watch, Hatred in the Hallways: Discrimination and Violence against Lesbian, Gay, Bisexual and Transgender Students in U.S. Public Schools, http://www.hrw.org/reports/2001/uslgbt/ (visited May 9, 2008); Pride and Prejudice: Working with Lesbian, Gay and Bisexual Youth (Margaret Schneider ed., 1997); *Flores v. Morgan Hill Unified School Dist.*, 324 F.3d 1130 (2003); *Massey v. Banning Unified School Dist.*, 2003 WL 1877841 (C.D. Cal., Mar. 28, 2003).

51. Anthony R. D'Augelli, *Lesbian, Gay, and Bisexual Development during Adolescence and Young Adulthood,* in Textbook of Homosexuality and Mental Health 267, 275 (Robert P. Cabaj and Terry S. Stein eds., 1996).

52. One well-known study found that "gay youth are 2 to 3 times more likely to attempt suicide than other young people. They may comprise up to 30 percent of completed youth suicides annually." Paul Gibson, *Gay Male and Lesbian Youth Suicide,* in 3 Report of the Secretary's Task Force on Youth Suicide, U.S. Dept. of Health and Human Services 3-110 (1989). Some recent studies have confirmed this finding, whereas others suggest that the disparity is far lower. See Ritch C. Savin-Williams, *Suicide Attempts among Sexual-Minority Youths: Population and Measurement Issues,* 69 J. Consulting & Clinical Psych. 983 (2001).

53. D'Augelli, *Lesbian, Gay, and Bisexual Development,* at 280.

54. See A. Damien Martin and Emery S. Hetrick, *The Stigmatization of the Gay and Lesbian Adolescent,* 15 J. Homosexuality 163 (1988). "These youth suffer from chronic depression and are at high risk of attempting suicide when the pressure becomes too much to bear. They may run away from home with no one understanding why. A suicidal crisis may be precipitated by a minor event which serves as a 'last straw' to the youth. A low grade may confirm for the youth that his life is a failure. An unwitting homophobic remark by parents may be taken to mean that the youth is no longer loved by them." Gibson, *Gay Male and Lesbian Youth Suicide,* at 3-120.

55. D'Augelli, *Lesbian, Gay, and Bisexual Development,* at 280.

56. See Cheshire Calhoun, *Sexuality Injustice,* 9 Notre Dame J. L. Ethics & Pub. Pol'y 241 (1995).

57. Martha C. Nussbaum, *"Secret Sewers of Vice": Disgust, Bodies, and the Law,* in The Passions of Law 46 (Susan A. Bandes ed., 1999).

58. Quoted in Mohr, A More Perfect Union, at 69.

59. John M. Finnis, *Law, Morality, and "Sexual Orientation,"* 69 Notre Dame L. Rev. 1049, 1052 (1994).

60. See, e.g., Congregation for the Doctrine of the Faith, *Letter to Bishops on the Pastoral Care of Homosexual Persons* (Oct. 1, 1985), 32 The Pope Speaks 62 (1987).

61. *Id.* A similar view can be found in *The Divine Institution of Marriage,* Newsroom of the Church of Jesus Christ of Latter-Day Saints, Aug. 13, 2008, available at http://newsroom.lds.org/ldsnewsroom/eng/commen tary/the-divine-institution-of-marriage (visited Sept. 19, 2008).

62. For examples from the writings of the Christian Right, which is the central agent of antigay political activity in the United States, see Didi Herman, The Antigay Agenda: Orthodox Vision and the Christian Right 25–59 (1997). For other illustrations, see Koppelman, Romer v. Evans *and Invidious Intent,* at 144 n.262.

63. One may object that the distinction between kinds of antigay attitudes that I am offering here is incoherent. Any condemnation of conduct will stigmatize those who are inclined to engage in that conduct. Yet not all potential wrongdoers are stigmatized as inferior. Even violent criminals are not despised in the way that gays are. Judge Richard Posner, no gay rights advocate, has acknowledged that homosexuals "are despised more for what they are than for what they do." Richard Posner, Sex and Reason 346 (1992). Try making sense of this statement as applied to murderers or robbers. Rape is a massive problem, but no derogatory epithet exists for (the very large number of) men who are sexually aroused by the thought of rape. The Catholic Church understands that when dealing with antigay prejudice it is dealing with something distinctively malign, not assimilable into its own condemnation of homosexual conduct.

64. See James Davison Hunter, Culture Wars: The Struggle to Define America (1991).

65. Quoted in *Boy Scouts of America v. Dale,* 530 U.S. 640, 643 (2000).

66. Position statement promulgated by the BSA in 1991, quoted in *id.* at 652 (majority opinion).

67. Another possible justification for the policy, ignored by the Court, is the canard that gay men are unusually likely to sexually molest their charges.

The organization disavows any such claim, although many members and even some leaders believe it. See Tracy Thompson, *Scouting and the New Terrain,* Washington Post Magazine, Aug. 2, 1998.

68. John Johnson, *Ballot Initiative Praising Scouts Is Latest Salvo in Heated Debate,* L.A. Times, Oct. 8, 2001, at B6; Peter Hong, *Scout Official Is Fired after Saying He Is Gay,* L.A. Times, Nov. 6, 2000, at A3.

69. As with Dale, the BSA expelled Lanzi without further inquiry. Telephone interview with Scott R. Ames, attorney for Mr. Lanzi, Nov. 26, 2001.

70. Quoted in *Dale,* 530 U.S. at 652.

71. Boy Scouts of America, Resolution of Feb. 6, 2002, http://www.scouting .org (visited Nov. 14, 2002).

72. One might use surveys to determine how the policy is interpreted by the American population, see Shari Seidman Diamond and Andrew Koppelman, *Measured Endorsement,* 60 Md. L. Rev. 713 (2001), but the policy's meaning is clear enough to make this unnecessary.

73. Quoted in Brief for Respondent, *Boy Scouts of America v. Dale,* 2000 WL 340276, at 3.

74. The Catholic Church's Congregation on the Doctrine of the Faith thus declares:

> An individual's sexual orientation is generally not known to others unless he publicly identifies himself as having this orientation or unless some overt behavior manifests it. As a rule, the majority of homosexually oriented persons who seek to lead chaste lives do not publicize their sexual orientation. Hence the problem of discrimination in terms of employment, housing, etc., does not usually arise.

Congregation for the Doctrine of the Faith, *Responding to Legislative Proposals on Discrimination against Homosexuals,* 22 Origins 174, 176 (Aug. 6, 1992).

75. Reply Brief for Petitioner, *Boy Scouts of America v. Dale,* 2000 WL 432367, at 10.

76. *Id.* at 11, quoting Nan D. Hunter, *Identity, Speech and Equality,* 79 Va. L. Rev. 1695, 1696 (1993).

77. See Herman, The Antigay Agenda 49–52, 96–97. Religious conservatives are split on this question. The Catholic Church has for years acknowl-

edged the existence of "homosexuals who are definitively such because of some kind of innate instinct." Congregation for the Doctrine of the Faith, *Declaration on Certain Questions Concerning Sexual Ethics* (1975), 21 The Pope Speaks 60 (1976), n.8.

78. See David B. Cruz, *Controlling Desires: Sexual Orientation Conversion and the Limits of Knowledge and Law*, 72 S. Cal. L. Rev. 1297 (1999).

79. These battles are described in Chapter 6.

80. See David McGowan, *Making Sense of Dale*, 18 Const. Comm. 121, 172–74 (2001).

81. See David I. Macleod, Building Character in the American Boy: The Boy Scouts, YMCA, and Their Forerunners, 1870–1920 212–14 (1983).

82. Even the U.S. military no longer does this, but rather justifies its policies on the basis of the anticipated reactions of nongay troops to the presence of gay soldiers. See Andrew Koppelman, *Gaze in the Military: A Response to Professor Woodruff,* 64 UMKC L. Rev. 179 (1995).

83. Between 2 and 5 percent of the male population is gay. See Richard Posner, Sex and Reason 294–95 (1992). Calculating from 3 million boys presently members of the BSA, the number of gay youth would range from 60,000 to 152,000. There is some evidence that the percentage is even higher among adolescents. See D'Augelli, *Lesbian, Gay, and Bisexual Development,* at 267–68.

84. Bishops Committee on Marriage and Family, National Conference of Catholic Bishops, *Always Our Children: A Pastoral Message to Parents of Homosexual Children and Suggestions for Pastoral Ministers* (1997), available at http://www.nccbuscc.org/laity/always.shtml (visited May 9, 2008).

85. *Doctors Say the Boy Scout Ban Will Increase the Rate of Suicide among Gay Youth,* The Advocate, June 19, 2001.

86. In 1960, Bob Jones Sr., the founder of the university, wrote (in a pamphlet defending racial segregation) that "no race is inferior in the will of God." Quoted in Mark Taylor Dalhouse, An Island in the Lake of Fire: Bob Jones University, Fundamentalism, and the Separatist Movement 155 (1996).

87. *Id.* at 5.

88. Although this chapter is not about law and makes no legal claims, the conclusion in the text does have legal implications. It indicates that the state may have a compelling interest in preventing a socializing agent as powerful as the BSA from discriminating against gay people. Legal inter-

vention, most notably the Civil Rights Act of 1964, appears to have played a powerful role in changing racist social norms. See Richard McAdams, *Cooperation and Conflict: The Economics of Group Status Production and Race Discrimination,* 108 Harv. L. Rev. 1003, 1074–82 (1995).

89. Albert O. Hirschman, Exit, Voice, and Loyalty (1970).

90. *Id.* at 124.

91. *Id.* at 98–105.

Chapter 6. Why Regulate the BSA?

1. William P. Marshall, *Discrimination and the Right of Association,* 81 Nw. U. L. Rev. 68, 96 n.166 (1986).

2. 530 U.S. at 659.

3. See Peter DeMarneffe, *Rights, Reasons, and Freedom of Association,* in Freedom of Association 145 (Amy Gutmann ed., 1998).

4. See generally Andrew Koppelman, Antidiscrimination Law and Social Equality (1996); Andrew Koppelman, *On the Moral Foundations of Legal Expressivism,* 60 Md. L. Rev. 777 (2001).

5. See Will Kymlicka, *Civil Society and Government: A Liberal-Egalitarian Perspective,* in Civil Society and Government 79 (Nancy L. Rosenblum and Robert C. Post eds., 2002).

6. Nan D. Hunter, *Accommodating the Public Sphere: Beyond the Market Model,* 85 Minn. L. Rev. 1591, 1634 (2001).

7. See Marshall, *Discrimination and the Right of Association,* at 94–96.

8. The same point could be made about political parties. A broad right of noncommercial association would not only hamstring antidiscrimination law; it would also render unconstitutional much of existing election law, which pervasively regulates party primaries. See Samuel Issacharoff, *Private Parties with Public Purposes: Political Parties, Associational Freedoms, and Partisan Competition,* 101 Colum. L. Rev. 274 (2001).

9. See 36 U.S.C.A. 30901 et seq. (2002).

10. David I. Macleod, Building Character in the American Boy: The Boy Scouts, YMCA, and Their Forerunners, 1870–1920 157 (1983); see 10 U.S.C.A. 772 (2001).

11. See 10 U.S.C.A. 2554 (2002) (equipment at BSA jamborees); 10 U.S.C.A. 4682 (2002) (Army equipment); 10 U.S.C.A. 7541 (2002) (Navy equipment); 10 U.S.C.A. 9682 (2002) (Air Force equipment); 14 U.S.C.A. 641

(2002) (Coast Guard equipment); see also 16 U.S.C.A. 539f (2002) (waiver of rental fees in National Forest System).

12. Chuck Sudetic, *The Struggle for the Soul of the Boy Scouts,* Rolling Stone, July 6–20, 2000, at 109. The support provided by the military is prodigious, involving the active assistance of nearly fifteen hundred uniformed members. See the army's press release at http://www.mdw.army .mil/news/AP-Hill_support_contributes_to_success_of_ Scout_Jamboree.html (visited Oct. 28, 2002).

13. Harold P. Levy, Building a Popular Movement: A Case Study of the Public Relations of the Boy Scouts of America 21 (1944).

14. Quoted in Brief for Respondent, *Boy Scouts of America v. Dale,* 2000 WL 340276, at 1.

15. *Id.* at 2.

16. *Id.* at 3.

17. Macleod, Building Character in the American Boy, at 178.

18. In its early days, the organization was as racist as the rest of American society. The founder of the Scouting movement, Lord Robert Baden-Powell, was frankly and unapologetically a champion of the white race, who as late as 1937 was eager to establish relations with the Hitler Jugend. Michael Rosenthal, The Character Factory: Baden-Powell and the Origins of the Boy Scout Movement 253–78 (1986). "The first American Boy Scout handbook included Baden-Powell's mnemonic device for 'N' in Morse code, a cartoon of a 'Nimble Nig' (the dot) chased by a crocodile (the dash)." Macleod, Building Character in the American Boy, at 212. The BSA's executive board decided that it would sanction no black troop without local council approval, and southern whites' veto was in constant use. One board member answered a critic by noting that to admit black boys "would lose us many white Scouts." Where there was no established council, the organization simply refused to register blacks. The Chief Scout Executive, James West, foresaw "great mischief . . . if we permit the organization of colored troops in some very small community, even with the consent of the superintendent of schools and other representative people. Suppose this small community eventually becomes part of a county council or district council—it would work havoc and be an unnecessary embarrassment to overcome." *Id.* at 213. In the North, there were black troops, but most were segregated. In some cases, segregation was imposed by the leadership. *Id.* at 213–14. Eventually, this policy was

relaxed, and in the late 1920s and 1930s (a time when the nation as a whole exhibited little concern about racial injustice) southern councils began to accept black troops, encouraged by a promotion campaign undertaken by the national office. "Stanley Harris, field executive for the South, estimated that by 1939 50,000 of the nation's 1,449,103 Boy Scouts were black." *Id.* at 214.

19. Levy, Building a Popular Movement, at 19.

20. Macleod, Building Character in the American Boy, at 156–57.

21. For a similar analysis from a very different perspective than the one I offer here, see Roderick M. Hills Jr., *The Constitutional Rights of Private Governments,* 78 N.Y.U. L. Rev. 144, 233–34 n.300 (2003).

22. This is emphasized in Epstein, *Constitutional Perils,* at 136–39.

23. The BSA has a total youth membership of approximately 2.9 million. See Chapter 5, note 1. Camp Fire USA reports a membership of "nearly 750,000," of whom more than half are girls and so are not eligible for membership in most of the BSA programs (girls can be involved in Venturing). See http://www.campfire.org/all_about_us (visited Apr. 25, 2008).

24. This point was made in conversation by Richard McAdams.

25. The Girl Scouts has recently reached near-parity, with 2.7 million youth members and 928,000 adult members; see http://www.girlscouts.org/who_we_are/facts/ (visited Sept. 19, 2008).

26. Steffen N. Johnson, *Expressive Association and Organizational Autonomy,* 85 Minn. L. Rev. 1639 (2001).

27. See Albert O. Hirschman, Exit, Voice, and Loyalty 98–105 (1970).

28. Rosenblum offers schism as the healthiest solution to the problem of discriminatory associations. See Rosenblum, Membership and Morals, at 170–71.

29. The New York board acted, in part, in response to a threat by the New York City government to prohibit its agencies from sponsoring Scouting activities. Eric Lipton, *A Challenge to Gay Ban by Scouts: 'Stupid' Policy, Say Local Scout Leaders,* N.Y. Times, Feb. 27, 2001, at A21.

30. See Laura Parker, Big Cities' Scout Leaders Pushing for Inclusion of Gays, *USA Today,* June 15, 2001, at 1A. Thus far, however, this movement has not succeeded in getting any modification of the national policy. The organization responded by enacting a resolution reaffirming the gay exclusion and stating that there is no local option to the contrary. See Boy

Scouts of America Resolution, Feb. 6, 2002, available at http://www.scou
ting.org/Media/PressReleases/2002/resolution.aspx (visited Sept. 24,
2008). The reformers are unlikely to succeed because conservative religious organizations are so strong within the BSA. "[R]eligious bodies
now sponsor 65 percent of all troops, compared with just over 40 percent
15 years ago." Benjamin Soskis, *Big Tent: Saving the Boy Scouts from Its
Supporters,* New Republic, Sept. 17, 2001. Of these, two-thirds are spon-
sored by the Catholic Church, the United Methodist Church, the Church
of Jesus Christ of Latter-Day Saints (the Mormons), the Lutherans, and
the National Council of Young Israel. Brief of Amicus National Catholic
Committee on Scouting et al. in Support of Petitioners, *Boy Scouts of
America v. Dale,* 2000 WL 235234, at 1. Of these, the Mormons "sponsor
more Scout troops and packs than any other religious or civic group in
the country." Lesley Stahl, *The Boy Scouts: Policy of the Boy Scouts to Disallow
Homosexuals into Their Ranks,* 60 Minutes, Apr. 1, 2001, CBS News Tran-
scripts. The Mormons are less than 2 percent of the U.S. population, but
more than 12 percent of all Scouts and 23 percent of all Scout troops.
Sudetic, *The Struggle for the Soul of the Boy Scouts,* at 105; Tracy Thompson,
Scouting and the New Terrain, Washington Post Magazine, Aug. 2, 1998.
"Almost all of the church's top leaders achieved the rank of Eagle Scout as
young men, and Mormon elders use the Boy Scout program as an integral
part of its youth ministry." Sudetic, *The Struggle for the Soul of the Boy
Scouts,* at 109. The Mormon leadership has a remarkably retrograde view
of homosexuality, one that sanctions even violent abuse of gay people and
that appears not to follow in any apparent way from Mormon theology.
See Katherine Rosman, *Mormon Family Values,* The Nation, Feb. 25,
2002.

31. See Sara Rimer, *Boy Scouts under Fire; Ban on Gays Is at Issue,* N.Y. Times,
July 3, 2003, at A19.

32. Ted Hill, Scout Council Member, quoted in Robert Siegel, Some Local
Boy Scout Chapters Are Losing Funding Due to the National Organiza-
tion's Ban on Gay Members, National Public Radio "All Things Consid-
ered," Aug. 22, 2003. The BSA has revoked the charters of some local
branches that refused to follow the national antigay policy. See, e.g., Lisa
Black and Courtney Challos, *Charters of 7 Cub Packs Not Renewed by Boy
Scouts, Oak Park Anti-Bias Code Conflicts with National Policy,* Chicago
Tribune, Jan. 26, 2001, at 3.

33. See Sydney E. Ahlstrom, A Religious History of the American People 659–65 (1972).

34. See *Out of the Fold? The Debate over Gay Ordination and Same-Sex Unions Poses a Critical Choice for Mainline Protestants: Embrace or Schism?*, Time, July 3, 2000; *Presbyterian Church Faces Split over Same-Sex Unions*, Buffalo News, Mar. 12, 2001, at B1; *Lutherans Address Same-Sex Unions*, Milwaukee Journal Sentinel, Jan. 16, 2001, at 1B; Caryle Murphy, *Confrontation Reveals Episcopal Split; Conservatives Attempt to Develop a Parallel, Supportive Church Hierarchy*, Wash. Post, June 2, 2001, at B9; John Rivera, *Deep and Difficult Differences Trouble Episcopalians in U.S.*, Baltimore Sun, Nov. 4, 2001, at 1F; Bruce Nolan, Methodist Split Not Seen as Answer, Bishop Says, but Church Still Deeply Divided on Gay Issue, New Orleans Times-Picayune, May 15, 2004. There is also a danger of schism over the issue within the worldwide Anglican Communion. See Stephen Bates, A Church at War: Anglicans and Homosexuality (2004).

35. See the society's accounts of its position in its international and U.S. Websites, at http://www.fsspx.org and http://www.sspx.org, and the sources collected at http://en.wikipedia.org/wiki/Society_of_St._Pius_X (all visited Sept. 19, 2008).

36. See John C. Ensslin, *Sanctuary St. Isidore Parish Flowers Despite Rift with Catholic Church*, Rocky Mountain News, Mar. 25, 2001, at 44A; see also the statistics enumerated at http://www.sspx.org.

37. See generally Jed Michael Silversmith and Jack Achiezer Guggenheim, *Between Heaven and Earth: The Interrelationship between Intellectual Property Rights and the Religion Clauses of the First Amendment*, 52 Ala. L. Rev. 467 (2001); Annotation, *Right of Charitable or Religious Association or Corporation to Protection against Use of Same or Similar Name by Another*, 37 A.L.R.3d 277 (1971).

38. There are, however, some significant religious groups that have used intellectual property rights to prevent schism. See, e.g., *Christian Science Bd. of Dirs. v. Nolan*, 259 F.3d 209 (4th Cir. 2001); *General Conference Corporation of Seventh-Day Adventists v. Perez*, 97 F.Supp.2d 1154 (S.D. Fla. 2000); *Church of Scientology International v. Elmira Mission of the Church of Scientology*, 794 F.2d 38 (1986).

39. See *Boy Scouts of America v. Teal*, 374 F.Supp.1276 (E.D. Pa. 1974), and cases cited therein (enjoining operation of "Havertown Sea Scouts").

40. Yael Tamir argues that the proper remedy for exclusion from dominant

associations is for the state to provide citizens with "a network of state-sponsored services that would lessen their dependency on the associations to which they belong." Yael Tamir, *Revisiting the Civic Sphere,* in Freedom of Association 214, 232 (Amy Gutmann ed., 1998). The regime that prevails after *Dale* is just the reverse of this: the quasi-official association is precisely the one doing the discriminating, and of course the state provides no alternative.

41. The naive identification of a cultural group's preferences with the expressed wishes of its leaders is critiqued in Madhavi Sunder, *Cultural Dissent,* 54 Stan. L. Rev. 495 (2001).

42. Rimer, *Boy Scouts under Fire,* at A19.

43. Telephone interview with Lewis Greenblatt, Oct. 22, 2002.

44. Chicago in fact had been attempting to enforce its human rights ordinance against the BSA when the *Dale* decision was handed down. See *Chicago Council of Boy Scouts of America v. City of Chicago,* 748 N.E.2d 759 (Ill. 1st Dist. 2001).

45. Their Supreme Court amicus brief stated:

> The ruling below threatens to fracture the Scouting Movement, destroying or at least severely diminishing BSA's ability to advocate and inculcate its values. If the appointment of scout leaders cannot be limited to those who live and affirm the sexual standards of BSA and its religious sponsors, the Scouting Movement as now constituted will cease to exist. *Amicus* The Church of Jesus Christ of Latter-day Saints — the largest single sponsor of Scouting units in the United States — would withdraw from Scouting if it were compelled to accept openly homosexual scout leaders. The other *amici* would be forced to reevaluate their sponsorship of Scouting, with the serious possibility of reaching the same conclusion.
>
> To be sure, the lower court's decision does not apply nationwide. Moreover, none of the *amici* has made a final decision as to how it might respond should the impact of the holding below be confined to New Jersey — whether to part company with Scouting altogether, to withdraw from Scouting just in New Jersey, or to take some other tack. But without doubt the rule established by the decision below threatens the existence of Scouting, at a minimum in New Jersey and probably throughout the United States. Given

the extent of their support, losing any of these *amici* as sponsors, whether in New Jersey or nationwide, would seriously disrupt BSA's ability to express and inculcate its message. The destruction or dismemberment of an expressive organization is perhaps the ultimate abridgment of the right of expressive association. That possibility was never faced in *Roberts* [or its successor cases]. It is very real here.

Brief of Amicus National Catholic Committee on Scouting et al. in Support of Petitioners, *Boy Scouts of America v. Dale*, 2000 WL 235234, at 25.

46. 156 U.S. 1 (1895).
47. McConnell, *Religious Freedom at a Crossroads*, at 194.
48. The BSA's Supreme Court brief emphasized the fact that "[t]roops are incontrovertibly small, closely knit groups." Brief for Petitioner, *Boy Scouts of America v. Dale*, 2000 WL 228616, at 40.

In addition to serving as a role model for Boy Scouting values, the adult leader is expected to serve as a "wise friend" to whom the Boy Scout can turn for guidance on all kinds of problems and issues, including sex. . . . Since Boy Scout Troops take many overnight camping trips and typically spend a week together in summer camp, there is a far greater degree of intimacy among members than would be the case in a group that met only for formal meetings. Indeed, a Scout leader may spend "more time actually interacting directly with a Scout than do his parents." When an 11 year-old boy away from home for the first time becomes afraid at night, skins his knee, or forgets his sleeping bag, he looks to his Scoutmaster for support.

Id. at 41. It also cited the right of parents to direct the upbringing of their children. See *id.* at 42–44. These arguments were of no avail in *Dale* because neither the intimate associations involved in Scouting nor the parents were the entities that decided to do the discriminating. That decision originated in a distant headquarters in Texas, without the participation or, in some cases, even the knowledge of local groups. But if the adult leaders of an individual troop wanted to exclude gays, they would have had a powerful claim.

49. See Michael W. McConnell, *Federalism: Evaluating the Framers' Design,* 54 U. Chi. L. Rev. 1484, 1493–94 (1987).

50. The classic exposition is Kevin Lancaster and R. G. Lipsey, *The General Theory of the Second Best,* 24 Rev. of Econ. Stud. 11 (1956).

51. Brief for Petitioner, *Boy Scouts of America v. Dale,* 2000 WL 228616, at 45.

52. *Id.* at 47.

53. See generally Andrew Koppelman, Antidiscrimination Law and Social Equality (1996); Nan D. Hunter, *Accommodating the Public Sphere: Beyond the Market Model,* 85 Minn. L. Rev. 1591, 1629–34 (2001); for a more skeptical view, see Nancy Rosenblum, Membership and Morals: The Personal Uses of Pluralism in America 166–90 (1998).

54. On the case for neutrality, see Andrew Koppelman, *Sexual and Religious Pluralism,* in Sexual Orientation and Human Rights in American Religious Discourse 215 (Martha Nussbaum and Saul Olyan eds., 1998), and Michael McConnell, *What Would It Mean to Have a "First Amendment" for Sexual Orientation?,* in *id.* at 234.

55. When it is made at retail, through the interpretation of particular statutes, it is not unusual for courts to find that particular associations are not reached by antidiscrimination laws. See Jay M. Zitter, Annotation, *What Constitutes Private Club or Association Not Otherwise Open to Public That Is Exempt from State Civil Rights Statute,* 83 A.L.R.5th 467 (2000).

Index

absolute rights, 72–73

adolescents. *See* youths

African Americans, 4, 6, 10–16, 17; libertarian right to exclude and, 1, 6, 7; low rate of hostility toward, 92–93; stigmatization of, 86, 88, 100; voting rights and, 14–16, 18, 23. *See also* antidiscrimination laws; racial discrimination; racism

airbag law, 39

airlines, 77, 81

Alabama, 18

Alito, Samuel, 60

Allport, Gordon, 92

Amar, Akhil, 146n.2

American Airlines, 81

American Boy Scouts, 110

American National Election Study, 92

Americans with Disabilities Act (1990), 58

Anglicanism, 108, 165n.34

antidiscrimination laws, 9–11; arguments for, 2–3, 10–11, 66, 76–77, 79–80, 89; burden of, 24, 76; compelling state interest and, 20, 41–42, 75, 76, 160–61n.88; *Dale* ruling implications for, x–xi, 24, 25, 26, 27–31, 40, 48, 51, 59, 64, 76, 113; desirable results of, xiii–xiv, 4, 64, 66, 107,

161n.88; economic interests and, 17, 45, 57, 68, 74; exemption policy proposed for, 76–77; expressive association doctrine and, 29, 33, 75–76; *FAIR* case and, 43–45, 145nn.36, 37; First Amendment scrutiny and, 58; forced association argument and, 17, 32; free association right vs. x, 1, 2, 16–17, 20, 51, 63–64; gay protection and, 57, 118; historical background of, 5–24; legitimacy of, 105–19, 160–61n.88; libertarian three-prong argument against, xii, 2–5, 64; limited scope of, x, xi, 23; message impairment by, 67–68; neolibertarian position on, 63, 65–80; private sector and, 11, 19–20, 99, 126n.71; religious groups and, 142–43nn.26, 27, 150n.56; strident private speech and, xii, 64. *See also* Civil Rights Act

antigay policies: BSA and, x, xi, xiii, 24, 26, 28, 31, 33, 34, 36–37, 51, 69, 77, 80, 81–82, 98–104, 105–6, 108–17, 110–12; Christian right and, 92, 101, 158n.62; military and, xi, 44, 46, 54, 136–37n.6, 143n.32, 153n.13, 160n.82; racial discrimination as analogous to, xiv, 45, 81, 82, 97–98, 105; reasons for state inter-